TABLE OF CONTENTS

CHAPTER 1: INTRODUCTION

The United States faces an uncertain and rapidly changing security future. Among the many challenges the U.S. military is likely to face in the coming decade are the requirements to project power into strategically important regions of the world and deter or defeat aggression by conducting military operations on land or at sea against capable opponents. Current strategic guidance acknowledges these requirements and directs the Joint Force to retain the ability to conduct such operations.[1] However, evolving strategic realities and the emergence of new threats and tactics, particularly those related to anti-access and area denial (A2/AD), will make retaining the ability to conduct forcible entry operations in the future a more important part of protecting U.S. national security and advancing U.S. interests in the world.

For the last several years, politicians and defense officials have debated how best to shape the military of the post-Iraq and post-Afghanistan era. This debate has taken place against the backdrop of significant economic challenges and associated demands for cuts in federal spending, including the defense budget. Frequently absent from these discussions is an acknowledgement of the need to sustain a robust forcible entry capability. However, the Joint Staff and senior defense officials must understand this requirement in order to ensure the Services retain essential capabilities now and develop others that may be needed in the future. In this way, the U.S. military will retain the ability to offer the President and Secretary of Defense feasible and acceptable options that span the entire range of military operations. In addition, a better understanding of the gaps between current capabilities and projected requirements will help joint and

---

[1] Barack Obama, *Sustaining U.S. Global Leadership: Priorities for 21st Century Defense* (Washington, DC: Government Printing Office, January 3, 2012), 4-5.

1

service programmers prioritize resources and make investments where they are most needed to ensure the best possible capability with the least risk to the Nation.

The ability of the future Joint Force to succeed in forcible entry operations may be at risk, not only because of emerging threats and new tactics, but also because the posture of the Joint Force and the resources available for national defense are going to shrink in the coming decade. This thesis will suggest several ways to mitigate that risk by emphasizing the capabilities that will be most essential to successful forcible entry operations in the future. Because forcible entry is among the most difficult and costly military operations to execute, many defense analysts today tend to downplay the need for such capabilities, preferring instead to believe that the future Joint Force will find other, less costly ways to accomplish its assigned missions. Particularly in challenging economic times, it may be tempting to indulge in the illusion that "putting your young men into the mud" is largely a thing of the past.[2] However, an over-reliance on digital technology, stand-off weapons, and precision engagements to fight future wars cleanly or at lower cost neglects many of the more important continuities of armed conflict, particularly with respect to its enduring political, moral, and psychological dimensions.[3] Failure to account for this reality could seriously weaken the Joint Force in future wars.

When considering joint forcible entry requirements in 2020 and beyond, certain questions emerge as central to the discussion: 1) What major challenges will future adversaries and the operational environment present the United States in 2020? 2) What does national strategy require of the Joint Force in terms of forcible entry capability?

---

[2] T.R. Fehrenbach, *This Kind of War: A Study in Unpreparedness* (New York, NY: MacMillan, 1963), 427.

[3] Herbert R. McMaster, "Continuity versus Change: Thinking about Future Armed Conflict" (lecture, National War College, Washington, DC, February 8, 2013).

3) What are the current and projected capabilities for forcible entry, and what gaps are most likely to exist in the future? 4) In light of this, where should the Department of Defense (DoD) focus its available resources to ensure it can meet the requirements of national strategy in 2020 and beyond?

Given that the U.S. military will not only shrink in the coming decade, but also be more CONUS-based than at any time since 1940, the ability to project military power will take on a level of relative importance greater than at any time in the last 60 years. This situation, coupled with the increased use of anti-access strategies and area denial tactics by a growing number of adversary states, requires the United States to not only retain the ability to get to the fight on some distant shore, but also conduct and sustain successful operations at great distances from home.[4] While securing the global commons and critical air or sea lines of communication is an essential precondition for operations abroad, *it is often only half the battle.* The other half--employing a military force on foreign soil to compel lasting change--is still usually necessary if the United States hopes to defend and advance its interests in a hostile world. Accordingly, as this thesis argues, *the United States military must significantly improve its ability to conduct joint forcible entry operations to meet the requirements of national strategy in the increasingly complex future operational environment.*

This chapter begins the analysis by looking briefly at joint forcible entry in historical context. Using "past as prologue" not only gives background and perspective to the discussion, it also provides a basis for comparing future requirements with past

---

[4] The term "anti-access" refers to those actions and capabilities, usually long-range, designed to prevent an opposing force from entering an operational area. The term "area denial" concerns those actions and capabilities, usually of shorter range, designed not to keep an opposing force out, but to limit its freedom of action within an operational area. For details, see U.S. Joint Chiefs of Staff, *Joint Operational Access Concept,* Version 1.0 (Washington, DC: Joint Chiefs of Staff, January 17, 2012), 6.

realities. Chapter 2 offers a snapshot of the future operational environment, summarizes the major trends that drive the need for forcible entry operations, and describes emerging threats and tactics with which the United States is likely to contend. This chapter also provides a projection of the size and overall force posture of the Joint Force of 2020 to frame the subsequent examination. Chapter 3 outlines the strategic requirements for forcible entry operations and provides four hypothetical vignettes set in the year 2020. Each vignette provides a plausible scenario in which the future Joint Force would require forcible entry as part of a larger U.S. or combined military operation. Chapter 4 summarizes the current and projected capabilities for forcible entry in the air, maritime, land, space, and cyber domains and discusses projected special operations capabilities. In addition, this chapter outlines the most important projected capability gaps for the future Joint Force. Chapter 5 completes the analysis by providing five recommendations for improving forcible entry capability in 2020 and beyond. The thesis then concludes by summarizing the findings and offering some final thoughts on the prospects for change.

This thesis will not address the more detailed aspects of capability development in each of the Services or the precise requirements within specific programs. For example, it will not describe the exact numbers and types of airplanes, missiles, armored vehicles, satellites, or maritime subsurface weapons that will be required in a given scenario or the length of time they will be needed to ensure success. Such a discussion is well beyond the scope of a paper of this length. Instead, these requirements will be treated conceptually, under the assumption that combatant commands and their service components will determine how much of each capability they actually require to accomplish future forcible entry missions.

Similarly, the question of the defense budget and its related processes will not be discussed in detail. Instead, the thesis will take for granted that, despite the coming age of austerity, some form of adapted budget process will remain in place; that DoD will have a smaller amount of total resources at its disposal; and that for every proposed addition or expansion in capability, a corresponding trade-off will have to be found elsewhere in the budget.

More broadly, this paper will not call into question the overall strategic focus of the United States as outlined in current national strategy. Although the existing set of national strategy documents requires the nation to accept significant risk, especially in the case of near-simultaneous overseas contingencies, any useful critique of national strategy would require its own separate discussion. Instead, strategic considerations will be discussed only to the extent that current strategy requires the future Joint Force to conduct forcible entry operations--a consideration, it should be noted, which has gone almost without mention in the contemporary debates about future capability.

This thesis uses a variety of primary sources including current national strategy documents, joint and service doctrinal publications, as well as observations and comments from significant defense personalities, both active and retired. Secondary sources include historical monographs, published reports from government agencies and think tanks, academic papers, and other works that provide background information, analysis of current political and military trends, and projections about future capabilities. In addition, these sources offer alternative points of view as well as insight into the current state of research on this subject. The intent is to provide a variety of sources from both military and civilian authors that contribute to an overall understanding of the issue.

Forcible Entry in Historical Context

Any discussion of future joint forcible entry must begin with an understanding of the term itself and some perspective on how this type of military operation has been used in the past. Current joint doctrine defines forcible entry as the "seizing and holding of a military lodgment in the face of armed opposition."[5] A lodgment is further defined as "a designated area in a hostile or potentially hostile operational area that, when seized and held, makes the continuous landing of troops and materiel possible and provides maneuver space for subsequent operations."[6] As a variant of this type of operation, doctrine also considers certain strategic raids conducted to seize an area temporarily and conduct limited operations followed by a planned withdrawal a form of forcible entry.[7] The latter are usually conducted using smaller, more mobile elements such as Special Operations Forces (SOF). In other words, forcible entry operations usually are not ends in-and-of themselves. Rather, they are more often the starting point for the "other half" of the battle that must take place after access is gained and forces are landed on foreign territory at the ends of extended air and sea lines of communication. Joint doctrine currently recognizes three forms of forcible entry: airborne operations, amphibious operations, and helicopter or fixed-wing air assault operations.[8] Depending on the situation and the military objective, Joint Force Commanders (JFC) can employ any combination of these forms of forcible entry as part of a larger campaign.

---

[5] U.S. Joint Chiefs of Staff, *Department of Defense Dictionary of Military and Associated Terms,* Joint Publication 1-02 (Washington, DC: Joint Chiefs of Staff, November 8, 2010, as amended through May 15, 2011), 144.

[6] U.S. Joint Chiefs of Staff, *Joint Forcible Entry Operations,* Joint Publication 3-18 (Washington, DC: Joint Chiefs of Staff, November 27, 2012), I-1.

[7] U.S. Joint Chiefs of Staff, *Joint Operations*, Joint Publication 3-0 (Washington, DC: Joint Chiefs of Staff, August 11, 2011), V-27.

[8] *Joint Forcible Entry Operations,* I-7.

Forcible entry operations have been among the most decisive military actions in history. They are also among the most challenging to conduct successfully. During *Operation Overlord* in World War II, Allied forces under command of General Eisenhower employed airborne, glider, and amphibious units to assault the northern coast of France and carve out a foothold on the European continent.[9] The initial landings enabled a build-up and subsequent offensive that liberated France, occupied Germany, and ended the war in less than a year. To a great extent, the Normandy operation succeeded because Allied commanders chose to offset their attack from strategic and operational objectives and strike where German forces were relatively weak. During *Operation Chromite* in the Korean War, Soldiers and Marines under command of General MacArthur conducted amphibious landings near the port city of Inchon on the west coast of Korea. The surprise attack behind enemy lines allowed U.N. forces to liberate Seoul, disrupt enemy lines of communication, and break out from the Pusan perimeter. In a matter of days, U.N. forces had begun a general offensive and completely reversed the entire momentum of the war.[10] A more recent example is *Operation Just Cause* in 1989 in which U.S. airborne forces conducted a series of surprise operations in a *coup de main* that removed Panamanian dictator Manuel Noriega from power, disbanded his defense forces, and returned the country to legitimate democratic rule.[11] Finally, in May of 2011 U.S. SOF used forcible entry at the outset of *Operation Neptune Spear*, the strategic raid into Abbottabad, Pakistan that killed Osama bin Laden.

---

[9] Albert Norman, *Operation Overlord, Design and Reality* (Westport, CT: Greenwood Press, 1952), 156-160.

[10] Roy E. Appleman, *South to the Naktong, North to the Yalu: The United States Army in the Korean War* (Washington, D.C.: Office of the Chief of Military History, Department of the Army, 1961), 571-572.

[11] R. Cody Phillips, *Operation Just Cause: The Incursion into Panama* (Carlisle, PA: U.S. Army Center for Military History, 2004), 46.

Given the high level of risk associated with forcible entry operations, they often impose excessive costs and sometimes fail. In mid-April of 1940, nearly 30,000 Allied troops landed on the west coast of Norway to defend the country against a German invasion.[12] Within days, the force was overwhelmed by German air and ground forces and the remaining survivors had to retreat and withdraw by sea. The failure had significant political repercussions and resulted in the resignation of Prime Minister Neville Chamberlain.[13] Two years later, Canadian and British forces were repulsed at Dieppe in an operation that cost the Allies nearly 4,000 casualties.[14] Even in operations that were ultimately successful, the cost of the attack has sometimes been so high that the outcome was a Pyrrhic victory, as in the German airborne assault on Crete in May of 1941 or the Allied landings at Anzio nearly three years later.[15]

The manner of conducting forcible entry operations has evolved significantly over the years. What has not changed much is the nature of war and the requirement it often imposes to seize an opponent's territory in the face of armed opposition in order to destroy his sources of power, impose terms, and end conflict. Accordingly, the next chapter will examine how the requirement for forcible entry is likely to evolve in the future based on projections about the operational environment, potential adversaries, and the likely posture of the Joint Force.

---

[12] J. L. Moulton, *The Norwegian Campaign of 1940: A Study of Warfare in Three Dimensions* (London, UK: Eyre & Spottiswoode, 1966), 249.

[13] Ibid., 245.

[14] Terence Robertson, *Dieppe: The Shame and the Glory,* (Boston, MA: Little, Brown, 1962), 386. In all, nearly two-thirds of the Allied forces taking part in *Operation Jubilee* were either killed or captured.

[15] Franz Kurowski, *Jump into Hell: German Paratroopers in World War II* (Mechanichsburg, PA: Stackpole Books, 2010), 165–166. German losses during the initial phases of *Operation Mercury* were so high that Hitler later told his senior staff he would never repeat such an operation.

CHAPTER 2: THE FUTURE OPERATIONAL ENVIRONMENT

The United States has dominated the world economically since 1915 and militarily since 1943. Its dominance in both respects now faces challenges brought about by the rise of powerful states. Moreover, the rise of these great powers creates a strategic landscape and international system, which, despite continuing economic integration, will possess considerable instabilities. Lacking either a dominant power or an informal organizing framework, such a system will tend toward conflict.[1]

Global Trends and Emerging Threats

Over the next ten years, major shifts in global economic power, population growth in developing countries, urbanization, continued resource scarcity, and the widening disparity between "haves" and "have-nots" will produce a security environment under increased stress.[2] Of the 196 countries in the world today, as many as 90 have the potential for failure as a consequence of their inability to meet basic needs or as a by-product of ethnic, cultural, or religious friction. In the past twenty years alone, there have been 50 ethnic wars, 170 border conflicts and two major wars involving extra-regional forces.[3] The uncertainty associated with rising regional powers, shifting alliances, and the proliferation of technologies will create a strategic landscape that presents the U.S. with a variety of challenges, but also a number of opportunities.

In addition, culture and identity will continue to be major drivers of conflict in the future. As a noted observer of international relations remarked some time ago, "the most important distinctions among people today are not ideological, political, or economic.

---

[1] U.S. Joint Forces Command, *The Joint Operating Environment (JOE) 2010* (Suffolk, VA: U.S. Joint Forces Command, February 18, 2010), 62.

[2] Brent Scowcroft, foreword to *Power and Responsibility: Building International Order in an Era of Transnational Threats* by Bruce Jones, Carlos Pascual, and Stephen John Stedman (Washington, DC: Brookings Institution Press, 2009), ix.

[3] C.J. Dick, *The Future of Conflict: Looking Out to 2020* (Camberley, UK: Conflict Studies Research Center, 2003), 3.

They are cultural."[4] In many places around the world, tribes, nations, racial and ethnic groups, as well as adherents to certain religious denominations are struggling to answer the basic questions of identity that have troubled mankind since the dawn of time. They want to know who they are--and who they are not; they want to know whom they are with--and whom they are against. As a result, cultural and religious differences have reemerged as major factors influencing cohesion and conflict across the globe.[5] As the events of the last several decades clearly illustrate, the principal religious and cultural phenomenon related to international conflict today is the rise and expansion of militant Islam.

Threats to U.S. national security will appear in many forms. Although near-peer competitors will continue to expand and modernize their militaries, it is unlikely that any great power will seek overt conventional confrontation with the U.S. in the next decade.[6] Rather, future enemies will oppose American interests using adaptive forces that operate in a decentralized manner to frustrate America's traditional advantages in firepower and mobility.[7] Their approach will emphasize a combination of *anti-access* strategies intended to deter effective U.S. diplomatic, economic, and military action while frustrating the ability to establish forward military presence or operate within a given theater; and *area denial* tactics to threaten local lines of communication and hinder tactical action.[8] These enemies will challenge U.S. national and political will with sophisticated information campaigns and cyber-attacks, while seeking to conduct

---

[4] Samuel P. Huntington, *The Clash of Civilizations and the Remaking of World Order* (New York, NY: Simon & Schuster, 1996), 21.

[5] Ibid., 20.

[6] *JOE 2010*, 62.

[7] Ibid., 66.

[8] U.S. Joint Chiefs of Staff, *Joint Operational Access Concept,* Version 1.0 (Washington, DC: Joint Chiefs of Staff, January 17, 2012), 6.

physical strikes within the homeland.[9] The global growth of military investments in offensive cyber capabilities, cruise missile technologies, long-range air defenses, and precision-guided artillery and rockets provides evidence for such an approach.

The most likely future conflicts will be against ideologically motivated opponents who employ a combination of traditional, irregular, and criminal tactics. These *hybrid threats* will be highly adaptive, globally connected, networked, and hidden in the clutter of local populations.[10] They will possess a wide range of new technologies, potentially including weapons of mass destruction. Their capabilities will include new weapons such as tandem-warhead rocket propelled grenades and advanced air defense systems that surpass those seen in Iraq and Afghanistan. They will continue to use a variety of improvised weapons and will likely employ technologies such as global positioning system jammers, homemade radio-frequency weapons, and rudimentary robotics systems to attack the U.S. reliance on technology.[11]

However, the U.S. cannot overlook the possibility of fighting a dangerous conventional opponent, including one armed with nuclear weapons. The political, economic, and military interests of a growing number of global actors are increasingly at odds with the U.S. and make conflict with them or their proxies a real possibility. The proliferation of doctrine and military equipment from Russia, China, and Iran to countries like North Korea and Venezuela, in addition to the effectiveness of non-state actors such as Hezbollah indicate the continued likelihood of battles that resemble conventional conflict, but may be more limited in time and space. Threat capabilities in such conflicts

---

[9] *JOE 2010*, 63.

[10] Ibid., 66.

[11] U.S. Army Training and Doctrine Command, Deputy Chief of Staff, G2, "Challenges to the Capabilities of the U.S. Army in 2020" (white paper, Fort Monroe, VA, January 17, 2011), 4.

could include high-volume indirect fire, advanced unmanned aerial systems (UAS) and anti-ship missiles, modern anti-tank weapons, top attack munitions, fourth generation chemicals, advanced air-delivered munitions, and electromagnetic weapons.[12] Opponents will employ these capabilities using new and modified tactics to gain advantages over U.S. and allied forces.[13]

As these patterns make clear, the land domain will remain a primary venue for future armed conflict. Because the U.S. retains significant overmatch in the sea and air, adversaries are more likely to challenge American interests on land where they can still compete effectively. Unlike in the air and sea, U.S. technology and modernization efforts have not deterred combat on the ground, which will offer adversaries in 2020 the ability to avoid many of America's relative strengths and achieve maximum effect at relatively low cost. Ground combat also allows them to test American resolve or deter action by presenting military situations that may require high levels of casualties and perseverance to solve.

Military operations over the next ten years will take place within unfamiliar cultures and among local populations. They will occur in urban settings and in harsh, inaccessible, lawless areas where the absence of security and governance locks competing factions in conflict. They will also take place in strategic chokepoints and along critical sea lines of communication. To succeed in such an environment, U.S. forces will have to deploy far from home and operate in an increasingly decentralized manner from forward locations and isolated outposts. Successful military operations may

---

[12] Fourth generation chemicals are a family of advanced nerve agents designed to be undetectable by standard NATO chemical detection equipment. For details, see Jonathan B. Tucker, *War of Nerves: Chemical Warfare from World War I to al-Qeada* (New York, NY: Pantheon Books, 2006), 479.
   [13] Andrew F. Krepinevich, Jr., *Seven Deadly Scenarios: A Military Futurist Explores War in the 21st Century* (New York, NY: Bantam Books, 2009), 285-317.

also demand long-term commitments at these extended distances using a wide range of interagency and non-military tools. In addition, every operation will be carried out under the unblinking eye of an ever-present formal and informal media that will give many local events global significance.

The U.S. military will also remain uniquely postured to assist in a wide array of stability and peacekeeping operations, humanitarian crises, and disaster relief efforts around the world. America's responses to the Indonesian tsunami, Hurricane Katrina, and earthquakes in Pakistan and Haiti are but a few recent examples of the type of missions the Joint Force may be called upon to support in the future as part of a whole-of-nation or international approach.

This strategic landscape makes a compelling case for the continued role of U.S. military power in the future, but it requires an approach that differs significantly from that of today. In the future, America's ability to exert influence and secure its interests using military force will continue to depend on its ability to project power from the United States to distant corners of the globe. However, military forces will also have to secure extended lines of communication, conduct forcible entry operations against capable enemies, and terminate conflicts decisively without the requirement for extended occupations or costly nation-building adventures. Such a strategy will require the United States to acknowledge and plan for a world in which increasingly capable competitors will challenge its access to areas of vital interest. In addition, the United States will have to work closely with friends and allies during peacetime to gain basing and over-flight rights, train allied military and security forces, build the capacity of reliable partners, and deter threats to security in distant regions of the world with a viable power projection capability. It will also require capable Third World allies who will "do the dirty work" of stabilizing the environment after conflicts are over, consistent with U.S. interests. In this way, U.S. forces will retain the ability to influence events abroad and advance American interests without forfeiting flexibility or courting strategic irrelevance in the 21st Century.

Anti-Access and Area Denial

Ever since the overwhelming success of the U.S. and its allies in the 1991 Gulf War, observers from around the world have speculated about how best to oppose the United States in future conflict. Among the earliest commentators on this subject was Brigadier V.K. Nair of the Indian Army. Shortly after the conclusion of Operation Desert Storm, Nair proposed a stratagem that would enable militarily inferior opponents to challenge U.S. access to regions of the world, threaten lines of communication, deny the unopposed deployment of carrier-based and amphibious task forces, and impose significant penalties on deploying or deployed forces.[14] Nair suggested that Third World countries could oppose the deployment of more powerful militaries using political, economic, and informational means to deny their opponents access to forward operating bases and sites to pre-position their logistics.[15] He also argued that militarily inferior powers should invest in a wide variety of long-range air defense systems and surface, sub-surface, and air-launched missiles that could hold a more powerful opponent at a distance beyond the range of his own carrier-based fighter aircraft, thus denying him the ability to operate effectively in a given operational area.[16] This general approach, conceived over two decades ago, offered a way for less-capable militaries to offset many

---

[14] V. K. Nair, *War in the Gulf: Lessons for the Third World* (New Delhi, India: Lancer International, 1991), 223-226.
[15] Ibid., 230.
[16] Ibid., 229.

of the traditional advantages of larger, more technologically advanced forces while imposing unacceptable costs on any military force that disregarded these emerging capabilities.[17]

In the years since 1991, these techniques have evolved and gained wider acceptance. Today, they describe some of the principal methods employed by less-capable militaries to deter more powerful opponents. The idea is not to confront an opponent directly with force, but to dissuade him politically or economically, threaten his ability to move military assets into an operational area, or position them in the most advantageous way by holding many of his high-value targets at risk. In current joint concepts, the term *anti-access* (A2) refers to "those actions and capabilities, usually long-range, designed to prevent an opposing force from entering an operational area."[18] In contrast, *area denial* (AD) concerns "those actions and capabilities, usually of shorter range, designed not to keep an opposing force out, but to limit its freedom of action within an operational area."[19] The two concepts complement one another in that anti-access concerns strategic and operational level approaches, while area denial focuses on operational and tactical level actions. The adoption of these approaches by states like China, Iran, and North Korea presents the United States with growing strategic and operational challenges that the Joint Force of 2020 must address in order to execute military strategy successfully.

The addition of A2/AD capabilities to the major military challenges facing the United States in the future has caused DoD to dedicate significant energy and resources

---

[17] Examples of "unacceptable cost" might include the sinking of a U.S. aircraft carrier on the open seas, or the shooting down one or more major transport aircraft, such as a C-5 or C-17.
[18] *JOAC*, 6.
[19] Ibid.

toward identifying how the Joint Force will deploy, execute, and sustain its military operations. Indeed, Brigadier Nair would no doubt be flattered that the United States is spending so much time and effort figuring out how to defeat the concepts he developed over 20 years ago. The efforts have been extremely creative and thoughtful. However, the wide attention paid to access challenges has caused many in the defense establishment to de-emphasize, at least implicitly, what one might call *the other half of the battle*--namely, those follow-on actions the Joint Force must often conduct in order to achieve the desired military and political end states. While in certain limited instances gaining access may truly be an end in-and-of itself, usually it is only a means to another end. It is in this context that forcible entry operations assume their central importance. If "getting there" truly is half the battle, the other half consists of those follow-on operations that strike at the sources of political, economic, and military power from which a conflict arises to defeat an enemy, alter those conditions in lasting ways, and impose acceptable terms of peace.

Posture of the Joint Force in 2020

Over the next seven years, DoD will face increasing pressure to downsize the U.S. military and relocate forces currently stationed overseas back to the United States. Despite the strategic implications of these changes, economic reality dictates that the federal government simply cannot continue to spend over a trillion dollars more each year than it takes in, and the defense budget will no doubt be the subject of intense scrutiny. Although any further downsizing will be a highly contentious political issue subject to numerous unknowns, it is likely that major cuts in force structure, procurement, and perhaps even readiness will be necessary to enable the federal government to return to a more sustainable level of spending that does not compromise the long-term economic health of the Nation. Depending on the strength of the economy, changes in federal tax law, and entitlement reform efforts over the next several years, DoD could easily be forced to reduce spending by as much as 25% over the next decade. Were this to happen, the military would have to reexamine its entire strategy and most likely adjust or eliminate a number of its current strategic commitments.

Assuming such an "Age of Austerity" did come, what might the Joint Force of 2020 look like, and how would it most likely be postured for the defense of the Nation, particularly with respect to the capability for joint forcible entry? Certainly, these questions are matters for discussion and decision by policymakers; however, absent clearly defined priorities--or perhaps even with them--the changes described below are all within the realm of possibility:

1) Nuclear Forces. Depending on the savings required, DoD will most likely have to reduce the nation's nuclear arsenal. In this regard, it may be possible to retain only the ballistic missile submarine (SSBN) leg of the current nuclear triad in its current strength while making significant reductions in the land-based intercontinental ballistic missile (ICBM) and strategic bomber legs of the triad. By 2020, the military could either retire or eliminate much of the missile and strategic bomber legs and rely instead on the most flexible and stealthy element of the triad for its nuclear capability. As current strategy suggests, such reductions could be done in such a way that they would not compromise the nation's overall nuclear deterrent.[20]

---

[20] Although its language is not specific, the 2012 Defense Strategic Guidance states, "It is possible that our deterrence goals can be achieved with a smaller nuclear force." For details, see Barack Obama, *Sustaining U.S. Global Leadership: Priorities for 21st Century Defense* (Washington, DC: Government Printing Office, January 3, 2012), 5.

2) Ground Forces. Under the current defense program, active duty ground forces are scheduled to shrink by more than 12% between now and 2017.[21] Active duty Army end strength is planned to go from roughly 567,000 to 490,000, while the U.S. Marine Corps will reduce in size from 202,100 to 182,100.[22] Over the next seven years, it is possible that the need for additional savings could drive these numbers even lower, with the Army ending up somewhere around 400,000 and the Marine Corps perhaps 150,000. In that case, DoD and Congress would also probably have to consider significant reductions in the Army National Guard and the Army and Marine Corps Reserves. Reductions of this size could easily cut the number of active Army airborne Brigade Combat Teams (BCT) from six to as few as three. The Army already plans to remove two of the four BCTs currently based in Europe, and the Marine Corps will remove most of its forces from Okinawa. Should additional ground force cuts be necessary (as outlined above), it is quite possible DoD could decide to remove the last two Army BCTs stationed in Europe and perhaps even the one stationed in Korea.[23] In addition, the number of active Marine regiments could be reduced by two or three. Given the proliferating missile threats in areas of importance around the world, ground-based missile defense capabilities will likely see little to no reductions.

3) Maritime Forces. The Navy would most likely have to reduce the number of Carrier Strike Groups (CSG) and their associated air wings from the current eleven to a

---

[21] United States Office of the Under Secretary of Defense for Acquisition, Technology, and Logistics, "Armed Forces Strength Figures for October 31, 2012," October 2012, http://siadapp.dmdc.osd.mil/personnel/MILITARY/ms0.pdf (accessed February 17, 2013).

[22] "20,000 Marines to be Cut, Pentagon Announces," *Marine Corps Times*, January 26, 2012, http://www.marinecorpstimes. com/news/2012/01/marine-20000-marines-to-be-cut-012612/ (accessed February 17, 2013).

[23] The current strategic focus on the Asia-Pacific region makes the removel of the Korea-based BCT unlikely. Even if it were inactivated, the U.S. would almost certainly retain headquarters and logistics forces in Korea that could support forward-rotating units or receive deploying forces in the event of a crisis.

more sustainable number like eight or nine. In addition, the Navy would probably have to make corresponding reductions in the number of its Expeditionary Strike Groups (ESG) and their associated amphibious assault, transport, and landing ships. The Navy and Marine Corps would also probably have to accept significant reductions in the acquisition of the B and C variants of the F-35. As a result, Navy end strength could drop from its current figure of around 317,000 to something closer to 275,000. America would certainly retain a capable two-ocean Navy, but it will almost certainly be leaner and more focused on its most critical missions.

4) Air Forces. The Air Force probably would have to reduce the number of attack aircraft by inactivating a number of its active duty strike wings and procuring smaller numbers of F-35 Joint Strike Fighters. Given the broad constituency for the F-35, the program will most likely survive, but even the A variant (intended for the Air Force) will probably have to be procured in significantly smaller numbers than currently planned.[24] The Air Force will also come under greater pressure to reduce transport aircraft such as the C-17 and variants of the C-130 as well as its aging fleet of close air support aircraft like the A-10. Cuts in Air Force personnel would most likely mirror those of the major airframes, perhaps reducing from roughly 332,000 to just under 300,000 with a proportionate share of the cuts likely in forward-based forces stationed overseas.

5) Special Operations Forces (SOF). Among all of the activities in DoD, SOF is likely to be one of the few that actually expands between now and 2020.[25] The demands of the ongoing global counterterrorism and counter-WMD efforts will most likely require

---

[24] Michael O'Hanlon, "What Cutting Defense Really Means," *Wall Street Journal*, January 29, 2013, http://online.wsj.com/article/SB10001424127887323277504578189883132379830 html (accessed February 18, 2013).

[25] Michael C. Bennett, "U.S. Special Operations Forces," (lecture, Joint Forces Staff College, September 14, 2012).

new systems, more personnel, and expanded authorities. As a result, U.S. Special Operations Command, its service components, and their assigned forces are likely to see sustained, if not expanded, spending on both personnel and advanced equipment. The posture of U.S. SOF will probably remain much as it is today, with perhaps some shifts in forces away from the greater Middle East to East Asia and Latin America.

6) <u>Intelligence, Space, and Cyber Activities</u>. The massive growth in intelligence spending that has taken place since 9-11 will probably not survive through 2020. In particular, the extensive redundancies among various agencies will likely become a target area for future savings. The sixteen major organizations commonly referred to as the Intelligence Community (IC)[26] may have to shed many of the thousands of new employees they have hired since 2001, while also consolidating their activities into a smaller and more governable number of agencies if their collective budgets are ever to be brought under control.[27] What may result is a smaller, but more focused intelligence apparatus that specializes in highly technical forms of signals intelligence along with effective human intelligence. At the same time, it is likely that the IC will continue to enjoy growth in the number and types of its various drone fleets and its advanced surveillance and monitoring capabilities. Space and cyber organizations are likely to provide new capabilities to the Joint Force in a variety of ways, but will also face the same fiscal realities. As a result, they may be able to sustain their current capabilities

---

[26] The sixteen agencies that constitute the IC, and the functions of each, were explained in detail to the author over an eight week JAWS elective course and during subsequent field research trips to the National Capitol Region.

[27] Dana Priest and William Arkin, "A Hidden World, Growing beyond Control," *Washington Post*, July 19, 2010, http://projects.washingtonpost.com/top-secret-america/articles/a-hidden-world-growing-beyond-control/ (accessed February 17, 2013).

without any major increase or decrease in resources, while shifting priorities to achieve greater capability in evolving cyber techniques.

7) <u>Joint Headquarters</u>. The Joint Force of 2020 will probably operate using a reduced number of unified combatant commands. In particular, DoD may choose to consolidate some of its current geographic combatant commands in order to focus on the most critical regions. In addition, it is likely to adopt a functional approach to directing joint warfare globally, as suggested in the most recent joint concepts.[28] Current proposals have envisioned reducing the number of geographic combatant commands to as few as three, or replacing them entirely with new interagency structures.[29]

8) <u>Other Possible Changes</u>. Finally, the Joint Force will probably face growing pressure to reduce the expense of its acquisition processes, make significant cuts in civilian personnel, trim pay and benefits for active duty military personnel, and revise the current medical and retirement programs to save additional money.[30] Although these changes would not directly affect the ability of the Joint Force to conduct forcible entry, they will most likely be a part of the environment in which the armed forces of the future will have to operate.

Although the changes outlined above are purely speculative, any observer of national politics and the Nation's fiscal situation would probably agree that many, if not all, of these changes are distinct possibilities between now and 2020. If policymakers

---

[28] Such an approach is already envisioned in the most recent capstone concept released by the Joint Staff. However, the document suggests that emerging threats and the operational environment, rather than fiscal necessity, will drive the Joint Force to such an outcome. For details, see U.S. Joint Chiefs of Staff, *Capstone Concept for Joint Operations: Joint Force 2020* (Washington, DC: U.S. Joint Chiefs of Staff, September 10, 2012), 6.

[29] Jeffrey Buchanan, Maxie Y. Davis, and Lee T. Wight, "Death of the Combatant Command? Toward a Joint Interagency Approach," *Joint Force Quarterly* 52, no. 1 (January 2009): 94, http://www.ndu.edu/press/lib/pdf/jfq-52/JFQ-52.pdf (accessed February 18, 2013).

[30] O'Hanlon, "Cutting Defense," http://online.wsj.com/article/SB1000142412788732327750457818988 3132379830.html (accessed February 18, 2013).

intend to maintain the readiness of the future force, that force will have to become smaller. Indeed, current strategy states that DoD will, "resist the temptation to sacrifice readiness in order to retain force structure, and will in fact rebuild readiness in areas that, by necessity, were deemphasized over the past decade."[31]

Such a force would probably be able to provide the Nation a capable nuclear deterrent, the ability to prosecute one major global contingency while executing a holding action in a second major contingency, and a heightened security posture in the homeland. Upon successful resolution of the first contingency, DoD could then reapportion selected assets to the lower priority operation as required. Such a force would also provide the ability to sustain global counterterrorism efforts while also supporting periodic stability, peacekeeping, humanitarian or disaster relief missions, assuming they are not concurrent with either major contingency. While much leaner than today's Joint Force, this military could probably still execute current national strategy, assuming it adopted more creative approaches and modified some of its organizations to operate more jointly and more efficiently. However, it would undoubtedly push the limits of acceptable strategic risk absent any reductions in its total global commitments.

Should this situation come to pass, the Joint Force of 2020 will be smaller and more CONUS-based than at any time since 1940. Given relevant projections about the operational environment and the likely adoption by adversaries of approaches that emphasize A2/AD, the need for U.S. forces to project power effectively will be even greater than today. In many cases, an effective military response to a crisis that threatens vital or important U.S. interests will require one or more forms of joint forcible entry at the ends of extended lines of communication. Indeed, depending on the circumstances,

---

[31] *Sustaining U.S. Global Leadership,* 7.

22

forcible entry may be the *only* real option if the U.S intends to defend or advance its interests around the world. In order to understand what the future may call for, it is necessary to discuss the strategic requirement for forcible entry in greater detail and examine some hypothetical future scenarios to see what they may require of the Joint Force in terms of such capability.

CHAPTER 3: STRATEGIC REQUIREMENTS FOR FORCIBLE ENTRY

Defeating adversary aggression will require the Joint Force to support national approaches to counter anti-access and area-denial strategies. Defeating these strategies will require Joint Force doctrine to better integrate core military competencies across all domains and account for geographic considerations and constraints. These core military competencies include complementary, multi-domain power projection, joint forcible entry, the ability to maintain joint assured access to the global commons and cyberspace should they become contested, and the ability to fight and win against adversaries.[1]

Strategic Imperatives

As outlined in the National Military Strategy, the future Joint Force requires robust capabilities to project power despite A2/AD challenges, counter terrorism and weapons of mass destruction, deter and defeat aggression, and conduct stability, humanitarian, and disaster relief missions.[2] Inherent in all of these operations is the potential requirement to conduct joint forcible entry and secure a lodgment to provide an area from which to direct local military operations, flow additional forces as necessary, assert and expand control over enemy terrain and resources, and sustain those operations over great distances, perhaps for extended periods of time. A brief examination of potential conflicts in areas of strategic interest to the United States suggests a number of plausible scenarios in which the United States could require this capability in the coming decade. This chapter will outline four such scenarios--all set in the year 2020--and discuss the possible forcible entry requirements associated with each. However, in order to introduce these scenarios properly, this chapter will describe briefly the development

---

[1] U.S. Joint Chiefs of Staff, *The National Military Strategy of the United States of America 2011: Redefining America's Military Leadership* (Washington, DC: U.S. Joint Chiefs of Staff, February 8, 2011), 8-9.

[2] Barack Obama, *Sustaining U.S. Global Leadership: Priorities for 21ˢᵗ Century Defense* (Washington, DC: Government Printing Office, January 3, 2012), 4-5.

of current thinking within and around DoD with respect to forcible entry as a strategic requirement.

Over the last decade, various organizations and defense experts have offered their visions of the military's future requirement for joint forcible entry. In January 2003, then-Deputy Secretary of Defense Paul Wolfowitz requested a department-wide review of forcible entry capabilities for the Joint Force. As part of this effort, he tasked the Joint Chiefs of Staff to explore Joint Seabasing concepts and related force capability packages in the Navy and Marine Corps.[3] Over the next two years, the RAND Corporation completed a thorough study of the matter and proposed an expanded set of capabilities that included specific enhancements to the Navy's Carrier Strike Groups (CSG) and Marine Corps expeditionary forces.[4]

More recently, a number of prominent think tanks have prepared reports outlining their vision of the future Joint Force. These organizations include the Center for Strategic and Budgetary Assessments (CSBA), the Institute for Defense Analyses (IDA), the Center for a New American Security (CNAS), and others. What is notable in the majority of these proposals is the lack of any significant discussion of joint forcible entry as a military requirement. Instead, many have chosen to emphasize the notion of "access" instead of that of "entry." For example, a recent essay by the CSBA suggests that America simply cannot afford to maintain an effective forcible entry capability and

---

[3] Robert Button et al., *A Preliminary Investigation of Ship Acquisition Options for Joint Forcible Entry Operations* (Arlington, VA: RAND National Defense Research Institute, May 16, 2005), xii. Joint doctrine defines sea basing as "the deployment, assembly, command projection, reconstitution, and reemployment of joint power from the sea without reliance on land bases within the operational area." For details, see U.S. Joint Chiefs of Staff, *Amphibious Operations,* Joint Publication 3-02 (Washington, DC: U.S. Joint Chiefs of Staff, August 10, 2009), V-51.
[4] Ibid., 72-73.

should instead adapt its military strategy to one of "assured access."[5] Under this modified strategy, the U.S. military would seek to defend American interests using an approach called "deterrence by denial."[6] The main purpose behind such a shift is to defend America more cheaply by focusing on capabilities that could deny a would-be aggressor his objectives without imposing excessive costs on the United States.[7] The CSBA approach owes a great debt to the important work that has been done, both inside and outside the Pentagon, on *Air-Sea Battle*. However, adopting a strategy of assured access as described in the *Air-Sea Battle* concept implies – at least indirectly – that the United States will no longer place emphasis on the ability to impose physical control over its opponents in distant locations, but rather focus on "offsetting strategies" that seek primarily to preserve U.S. access.[8] Such an approach assumes a significant amount of strategic risk and could easily fall short in many situations where physical control of an enemy or his resources is needed to defend or advance important U.S. interests.

In early 2012, the Joint Chiefs of Staff published the *Joint Operational Access Concept* (*JOAC*) to describe their vision for how the future Joint Force can counter the growing A2/AD capabilities of states such as China and Iran. The concept advocates a number of important adaptations to joint operations. These include a more extensive preparation of the operational area emphasizing the use of cyber and space capabilities; the use of multiple, independent lines of operation against an enemy; attacking A2/AD capabilities in depth, rather than rolling them back from a perimeter; and the achievement

---

[5] Andrew F. Krepinevich, Jr., "Strategy in a Time of Austerity: Why the Pentagon Should Focus on Assuring Access," *Foreign Affairs* 91, no. 6 (November-December 2012): 58.
[6] Ibid., 65.
[7] Ibid.
[8] Jan van Tol et al., *AirSea Battle: A Point of Departure Operational Concept* (Washington, DC: Center for Strategic and Budgetary Assessments, 2010), 9-10.

of what it calls "local domain superiority" over the enemy.[9] While placing considerable

emphasis on a strategy of assured access, the *JOAC* allows that the future Joint Force

must also be able to conduct forcible entry operations ranging in scope "from raids and

other limited-objective operations, to the initiation of sustained land operations."[10]

Nevertheless, the concept's distinct focus on actions to secure access to the "global

commons" defines a strategic approach very similar to that outlined by the CSBA.[11]

The first major concern with a strategy that emphasizes access is its tendency to

cede the strategic and operational initiative to America's adversaries. Among those who

have recognized this fundamental problem is Frank Hoffman, who several years ago

observed the following with respect to forcible entry capability:

> The ability to quickly introduce maneuver forces and undertake decisive
> operations enables the joint force commander to seize the initiative and
> alter the parameters of a conflict. By massing the effects of precision fires
> and distributed forces, he can retain the initiative and force the opponent
> to react.[12]

Hoffman later continued:

> By their combinations of operational maneuver and firepower, forcible
> entry operations also present a range of dynamics and dilemmas to
> adversaries. The enemy commander can respond to our deep maneuver by
> concentrating his units, which exposes them to our joint fires. If his forces
> remain fixed in place, they can be isolated and eliminated in detail.
> Whatever the enemy decides, he faces a series of dilemmas for which he
> will have fewer and fewer options.[13]

---

[9] U.S. Joint Chiefs of Staff, *Joint Operational Access Concept,* Version 1.0 (Washington, DC: Joint Chiefs of Staff, January 17, 2012), 17.

[10] Ibid., 35.

[11] The *Joint Operational Access Concept* defines the global commons as "areas of air, sea, space and cyberspace that belong to no one state." For further details, see *JOAC*, 1.

[12] Frank G. Hoffman, "Forcible Entry Is a Strategic Necessity," *Proceedings* 130, no. 11 (November 2004): 2-2, http://web.ebscohost.com/ehost/detail?sid=2781dc5f-b184-44c9-a2e404d5d616263d%40sessio nmgr13&vid=1&hid=8&bdata=JnNpdGU9ZWhvc3QtbGl2ZSZzY29wZT1zaXRl#db=a2h&AN=15035504 (accessed September 13, 2012).

[13] Ibid.

If the United States is interested in retaining the strategic and operational initiative in the years to come, it must give thoughtful consideration to the distinction between a strategic approach that seeks primarily to assure access and one that seeks to threaten a potential enemy's territory and resources at the time and place of the United States' choosing.

A second major concern with a strategy focused on ensuring access is its implicit assumption that access alone will be adequate to resolve conflict or sustain a subsequent peace. In this context, it is important to recall the centrality of the land domain in armed conflict. While securing critical sea and air lines of communication is an essential part of any military campaign, more often than not *is it only half the battle*. Failing to maintain such lines can easily cause a military campaign to fail; however, merely securing them is rarely enough to accomplish the military objective. As British naval historian Sir Julian Corbett observed many years ago, "since men live upon the land and not upon the sea, great issues between nations have always been decided – except in the rarest of cases – either by what your army can do against your enemy's territory and national life, or else by the fear of what the fleet makes it possible for your army to do."[14]

More fundamentally, any strategy that focuses on access or deterrence by denial will often fail to appreciate (much less resource) the ability to exercise positive control and impose one's will on a capable enemy.[15] Implicitly or explicitly, such a strategy could easily neglect the fact that landpower is sometimes the only effective tool available to policymakers when faced with issues of great national importance. Any number of future strategic challenges may require a military force to impose America's will upon an enemy by altering or removing the sources of political, economic, or military power from

---

[14] Julian S. Corbett, *Principles of Maritime Strategy* (Mineola, NY: Dover Publications, 2004), 14.
[15] Lukas Milevski, "*Fortissimus Inter Pares:* The Utility of Landpower in Grand Strategy," *Parameters* XLII, no. 2 (Summer 2012): 10.

which he draws his strength.[16] When that happens, often the only way to accomplish the task is to enter the enemy's territory and exercise positive control over his government and population for as long as the mission requires. It is for this reason that the U.S. military must retain the ability to conduct effective joint forcible entry operations in the future. In the final analysis, Rear Admiral J.C. Wylie was surely correct when he observed, "The ultimate determinant in war is the man on the scene with the gun. This man is the final power in war. He is control. He determines who wins."[17]

The four vignettes that follow present a series of plausible scenarios in which the use of joint forcible entry could be necessary in the future. The first concerns power projection against a nuclear-armed Iran that has attempted to assert control over the Straits of Hormuz. The second describes how forcible entry operations could support counterterrorism and counter-WMD operations against radical elements inside an imploded Pakistan. The third envisions a renewed Korean War in which the United States and China have chosen to play active but limited roles. Finally, the fourth vignette describes how forcible entry could be part of stability operations in a war-torn and chaotic Nigeria that has requested international assistance to separate warring factions and provide humanitarian assistance. Each vignette presents unique requirements, but clearly more than one could arise simultaneously in the future. For this reason, it is important to consider not only the specific requirements of any one scenario, but also the aggregate requirement that two or more such scenarios might produce.

---

[16] Antulio J. Echevarria, II, "Rethinking the American Way of War and the Role of Landpower," U.S. Army War College Strategic Studies Institute, article posted September 10, 2012, http://www.strategicstu diesinstitute.army.mil/index.cfm/articles/Rethinking-the-American-Way-of-War-and-the-Role-of-Land power/2012/09/10 (accessed September 25, 2012).

[17] J. C. Wylie, *Military Strategy: A General Theory of Power Control* (Annapolis, MD: Naval Institute Press, 1989), 46, 72.

Iran 2020: A Nascent Nuclear Power Closes the Straits of Hormuz

By the year 2020, Iran has developed a modest nuclear weapons capability, despite strong international opposition and painful economic sanctions. Iran has also produced the Shahab-4 missile system, which is capable of delivering a nuclear device to a range of some 3100 miles. Countries around the world engage in loud and sustained protest, but a threatened attack by Israel and the United States to stop or delay the nuclear program never comes. Persuaded by U.S. and international inaction that its nuclear capability will deter any direct attack in the future, and in the belief that the time has finally come to assert its regional hegemony, Iran declares the Straits of Hormuz to be under Iranian control and uses its naval forces and coastal defenses to close the straits to all commerce not approved by Tehran. In response, the U.S. and its allies approve and deploy a combined joint task force to re-open the straits by force, but without crossing the nuclear threshold. The allied force is not only required to open the straits; it must also secure the adjacent terrain from which Iran can influence or interrupt navigation, and destroy Iranian offensive capabilities in order to re-establish international commerce in the Persian Gulf.

Vignette 1: Power Projection

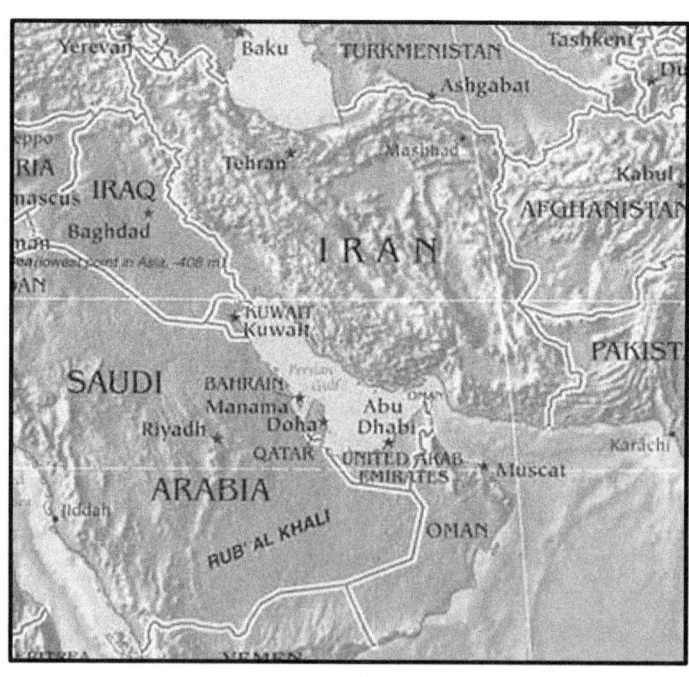

Figure 1: Iran 2020

In this first hypothetical vignette set in the year 2020, the United States and its

allies are confronted with the challenge of forcing opening the Straits of Hormuz, which

have been closed by a nuclear-armed Iran. Except for tacit support from Russia, which stands to benefit significantly from higher oil prices, Iran is largely alone against the world. However, its actions find a measure of support from Iraq, Syria, and several lesser global actors, all of whom seek to damage the power and credibility of the United States. Opposing Iran are the countries of the Gulf Cooperation Council (GCC), assisted by the United States and its NATO allies, India, Australia, and Japan. China and Pakistan remain neutral. As the crisis develops, coalition countries seek basing and over-flight rights in and around the region and posture themselves for conflict.

The U.S.-led coalition must consider its options very carefully in order to avoid a nuclear war. However, it cannot secure the straits or remove Iran's capability to interdict commerce in the Gulf without eliminating Iranian naval power in and around Bandar Abbas and destroying the extensive missile installations on the Iranian coast. To ensure the threat is removed in a lasting way, the coalition receives U.N. endorsement to establish and enforce an international demilitarized zone (DMZ) along the northern coast of the Gulf extending 100 miles to the east and west of Bandar Abbas.

The coalition deploys a combined force to the Gulf region and begins military operations to re-open the straits. In a matter of weeks, Iranian air and naval capability are destroyed, along with the coastal missile defenses. With air and sea superiority, the coalition then assembles an international force to establish the DMZ. Iran attempts to widen the conflict by launching missiles at the GCC states and Israel, but most are destroyed by friendly missile defenses, and none are nuclear. The coalition then deploys a combined force to occupy the Iranian coast and enforce the international DMZ. Supported by U.S. Carrier Strike Groups, Gulf-based U.S. air power, and coalition air forces, two Marine Expeditionary Brigades land on the Iranian coast west of Bandar

Abbas. Army Ranger and airborne forces conduct airborne assaults offset from the mainland air and port facilities near Bandar Abbas, and an international force lands on the coastal strip to the east. While the necessary air and sea ports are being brought under control, coalition air power interdicts all Iranian military forces attempting to move south. A combination of intelligence activities, SOF, and cyber-attacks disrupts the Iranian nuclear program and precludes its use. Follow-on U.S. forces then arrive in southern Iran by sea with reinforcing armor and mechanized units that strike out from Bandar Abbas to establish defensive positions and enforce the DMZ.

After a period of months, additional international forces arrive and begin to assume responsibility for portions of the DMZ. Throughout the operation, coalition messaging makes clear that if Iran will renounce its nuclear weapons program, give up its fissile materials, and guarantee international control of commerce on the straits, then the coalition force will depart. Over time, Iran's isolation and the loss of its oil-related revenue cause growing domestic unrest. The threat to the regime eventually compels Tehran to acquiesce. Within weeks, international engineers arrive to begin dismantling Iran's nuclear program. At the same time, coalition countries and Iran sign an agreement by which military forces will depart one year after the nuclear program is removed.

As this vignette suggests, Iran is not likely to start a nuclear war over the Straits of Hormuz. However, until such time as the U.S. and its allies actually commit forces and compel an outcome that changes the long-term power dynamic, Iran still retains the initiative and continues to blackmail the world. What changes the dynamic is the use of forcible entry to seize the initiative and alter the basic power equation. Once Iran's ability to control the straits and its southern coast is forcibly removed, the initiative passes to the U.S. and its allies. Only then can the coalition enforce an outcome consistent with international law and supportive of their interests.

The critical military capabilities required to succeed in such an operation include the ability to deploy rapidly, achieve air and sea superiority, defeat A2/AD systems, project military power onto foreign soil, and defend against a capable attacking enemy. To do this, the Joint Force must be able to secure lodgments using a combination of amphibious, air assault, and airborne units. Then it must immediately flow mobile, armored forces and material forward to exploit outward from those lodgments in order to establish and enforce the DMZ. Some military planners may believe that the objectives of this operation could be achieved without entry operations, much less forcible entry. However, without controlling the land that dominates both sides of a strategic waterway, a strictly punitive expedition is not likely to change the status quo significantly.

Pakistan 2020: A Failed State Loses Control of its WMD

Pakistan has endured six years of growing domestic strife. Four successive governments have failed since the withdrawal of NATO forces from Afghanistan in late 2014. Despite intense security and international scrutiny, two elections in a row suffer from widespread fraud, and violence across the country escalates dramatically. Populist and Islamist political parties scramble for power and the country descends into chaos. An attempted military coup fails, and many of the country's senior military officers are assassinated by Islamist militias. The *Jamiat Ulema-e-Islam* seizes power and declares a new Islamic state in Pakistan. A state of civil war ensues, and militia forces attack military facilities across the country, including several in which nuclear weapons are stored. As a result, at least 40 of the estimated 110 nuclear devices in Pakistan fall into the hands of radical Islamist groups. India mobilizes its armed forces and threatens to invade Pakistan in order to restore the proper civil authorities to power. Faced with no acceptable alternative, the U.S. agrees to conduct a series of precision military incursions into Pakistan to secure the loose nuclear materials and preclude a new Indo-Pakistani war.

Vignette 2: Counterterrorism and Counter-WMD

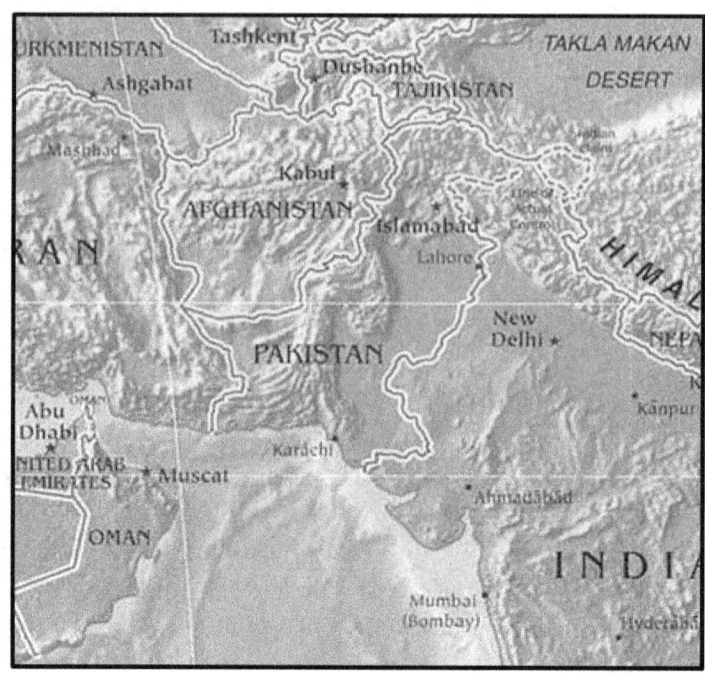

Figure 2: Pakistan 2020

In this second vignette, Pakistan has lost control of its nuclear arsenal. Radical Islamists have taken over the government and hundreds of militiamen armed with light and medium weapons have occupied a number of military facilities, including two that store nuclear weapons. Fully expecting a response, the militiamen fortify their positions in anticipation of an armed attack. Militants repel an initial assault by the Pakistani Army at one facility. In response, U.S. intelligence contacts the Pakistani directorate for Inter-Services Intelligence (ISI) and offers assistance to end the crisis and preclude moves by India that threaten war. U.S. SOF are directed to execute a series of simultaneous raids to defeat the militiamen, secure the nuclear materials, and retain control of them until they can be returned to legitimate Pakistani control. If unable to return the weapons safely, the force is ordered to disable or destroy them in place. Within days, U.S. special operating forces deploy to an American carrier in the Arabian Sea and other undisclosed locations inside Pakistan in order to prepare for the strike.

34

The locations of the raids require U.S. forces to conduct forcible entry by airborne and helicopter insertion in close coordination with commandos of the Pakistani Special Service Group (SSG), who attack by both air and ground movement. In all, a force equivalent to three battalions in strength assaults the militant positions. Assisted by extensive airborne firepower and real-time surveillance from U.S. national assets, the combined force overwhelms the militants and retakes control at two bases. Owing to incomplete intelligence and the need to strike quickly, the third SOF element finds out only after insertion that it faces a militant force more than twice as large as it expected. Although able to secure a portion of the third facility, the attacking force suffers heavy casualties and requires reinforcements to succeed. Pakistani and U.S. SOF then deploy another battalion-sized commando force, supported by heavy armor on the ground, to assist the attack. Within 24 hours, the force secures the third base. Eventually, SOF forces at the two bases with nuclear materials locate all of the nuclear weapons and, assisted by their Pakistani counterparts, disable these weapons permanently.

Meanwhile, word of the attack spreads and massive crowds of angry Pakistani civilians and militants begin to gather and move toward the three bases. The crowds demand that any Americans involved in the attacks be handed over to them for trial and execution under Islamic law. Over the course of the next day, additional Pakistani military forces arrive by ground movement and reinforce the bases, but with the angry mobs steadily growing, ground extraction of the American force is out of the question. Instead, they must be extracted by helicopter to an alternate staging location from which they can transfer onto cargo aircraft for movement out of the country. The U.S.-Pakistani SOF force secures and holds the perimeters of all three bases for another two days, and under cover of darkness, the American force removes small but critical nuclear materials and departs for home.

This vignette presents what could rightly be called a "nuclear nightmare" scenario in which speed of response is the critical factor. U.S. and Pakistani SOF must resolve the crisis in a matter of days, not weeks or months. In addition, U.S. involvement is necessary to delay unilateral military action by India and preclude a possible move toward a regional war. Although the Pakistani military has an adequate immediate response force, U.S. forces provide the intelligence, precision firepower, and political cover that enable to operation to succeed. The ability to conduct forcible entry into a hostile area, seize essential materials, and conduct a successful extraction proves critical.

The critical military capabilities required to succeed in such an operation include the ability to deploy rapidly, insert one or more battalions worth of highly trained forces into a hostile environment for direct action, conduct sensitive site exploitation, sustain the operation from a distance, and extract the force upon completion of the mission. To succeed in such missions in the future, the Joint Force must retain a robust and effective SOF capability able to operate on short notice all-around the world. In addition, the U.S. must sustain its ability to transport such a force secretly, supplement it with conventional capabilities, provide airborne fire support and control, and feed real-time intelligence to forward-deployed forces. These capabilities will continue to prove invaluable, particularly as a growing number of Third World countries continue to move toward or achieve a nuclear capability. Absent these capabilities, the U.S. military may be unable to offer the President effective options for dealing with "loose nuke" scenarios, whether in Pakistan or other countries that possess--or aspire to possess--nuclear weapons.

Korea 2020: A Second War on the Peninsula

By the year 2020, relations between North and South Korea deteriorate to a new post-war low. North Korean dictator Kim Jong-un intensifies his rhetoric and claims two island groups along the maritime border with South Korea. Occasional artillery duels take place, and a South Korean vessel is torpedoed by a North Korean submarine. Later, numerous infiltration tunnels are discovered along the DMZ. By this time, U.S. forces have largely withdrawn from the peninsula, and what remain are only headquarters and logistics troops. Faced with yet another year of famine and growing domestic unrest, Kim calls on his people to end the division of their country and unite Korea under his leadership. Without formally consulting China, Kim launches an all-out attack. Initially, South Korean forces falter, but within a week they have blunted the attack. South Korea immediately calls on the U.S. to honor its defense pact and come to its assistance in reuniting Korea by force. The United States and Pacific allies return to the peninsula with the mission to help South Korean forces capture Pyongyang and end the regime of Kim Jong-un while securing many of the nuclear sites and materials in North Korea.

Vignette 3: Deter and Defeat Aggression

Figure 3: Korea 2020

In a third plausible 2020 scenario, North Korea attacks South Korea in a surprise move that startles the world. Faced with a resumption of hostilities, the United States and South Korea's other allies honor their commitments and come to the defense of the

Republic of Korea (ROK). However, the situation in the early days of the Second Korean War is much different than 70 years before. In fact, ROK forces are able to blunt the initial attacks largely on their own without losing a significant amount of territory. Seoul and other major cities are badly damaged in places, but remain under ROK control.

Flush with its initial success, the ROK resolves to take the offensive, end the regime of Kim Jong-un, and reunify the country.[18] World opinion strongly supports South Korea, but at the same time, the U.S. and the ROK open communications with China in an effort to prevent drawing Beijing into the war. Clearly exasperated with its junior partner, China secretly agrees to remain out of the war if U.N. forces do not approach or militarize the border with Manchuria.[19] Shortly thereafter, ROK forces cross the 38th parallel, and within several weeks they arrive in Pyongyang. Kim Jong-un abdicates and the totalitarian regime collapses. As Korea sorts out how to reunify after 70 years of division, U.N. forces move quickly to seize North Korea's fissile materials before they can be removed, hidden, or proliferated.

A renewed war in Korea would most likely require U.S. forces to employ forcible entry capabilities in at least two ways. The first is a conventional form of forcible entry from the sea that uses amphibious forces to land behind enemy formations in order to threaten their lines of communication and enable inland offensive operations up and down the peninsula. Success in such operations would require air superiority, adequate assault craft for at least two brigades of ground forces, and protection capabilities to

---

[18] The goal of reunification in the event of war is in keeping with longstanding Republic of Korea policy. For details, see Kristen Chick, "South Korea says it will prepare for unification with North," *The Christian Science Monitor,* December 29, 2010, http://www.csmonitor.com/World/terrorism-security/ 2010/1229/South-Korea-says-it-will-prepare-for-unification-with-North (accessed February 27, 2013).

[19] Choi Hyung-kyu and Kim Hee-jin, "'Give up on Pyongyang,' says China insider," *Korea JoongAng Daily*, March 2, 2013, http://koreajoongangdaily.joinsmsn.com/news/article/article.aspx?aid=2967922& cloc= joongangdaily%7Chome%7Ctop (accessed March 3, 2013).

defeat enemy airpower, rockets, artillery, and mortars. In addition, successful forcible entry would require ground forces to retain enough mobile protected firepower systems to enable movement inland by otherwise unprotected light infantry forces.

The second major way forcible entry could be critical in a future Korean War is with respect to regime collapse and the need to secure sensitive nuclear materials. North Korea has a multitude of facilities tied to its nuclear program, many of which are located inland in isolated areas and difficult terrain. U.S. forces may require airborne or helicopter-borne forces to assault and secure these remote sites, especially in instances where remnants of the former regime or political die-hards refuse to surrender. Although such resistance would probably diminish over time, it may be necessary to conduct multiple battalion-sized operations simultaneously. In this case, U.S. air power could provide an outer cordon while ground forces provide an inner cordon and secure the sites.

The critical military capabilities required to succeed in such an operation would include the ability to achieve local air and maritime superiority, defeat enemy drones, and employ amphibious forces to exploit inland rapidly to threaten or cut off enemy lines of communications. Success would also require extensive surveillance and intelligence of all possible nuclear sites, robust theater airlift, effective joint fires, and at least several battalions of ready airborne forces specialized in weapons detection, explosive ordinance disposal, and a variety of engineering skills. In addition, once the sensitive nuclear sites are secure, ground forces would have to move rapidly over difficult, compartmentalized terrain--as they would in a movement to contact--in order to link up with and reinforce the forward deployed entry forces. Without this type of capability, U.S. forces would be compelled to accept considerable risk with respect to the security of these sites.

Nigeria 2020: Descent into Chaos

Militant Islam has significantly increased its presence in the northern three-quarters of Africa's most populous and oil-rich country. The capital of Abuja has seen more than two years of conflict as Islamist groups assume control of more and more sectors of society and the economy. Supported militarily by groups in Niger, Chad, and Sudan, the Islamists uproot and kill thousands of Nigerian Christians, causing a major humanitarian crisis. At the same time, Islamic pirates begin to disrupt trade and commerce along the Niger Delta and the coast of Nigeria. Oil shipments are suspended due to the chaos, and worldwide prices spike due to decreased production. Unable to quell the violence, Nigeria requests international assistance to help stabilize the country. As part of a UN-sanctioned, multinational peace enforcement mission, the United States deploys a joint force to conduct stability operations and provide humanitarian assistance in southeastern Nigeria. British and French forces operate in central and northern Nigeria, along with forces from various African Union countries. Because hostile groups are still active throughout the country, US forces must build a lodgment from which they can conduct operations.

Vignette 4: Stability and Humanitarian Operations

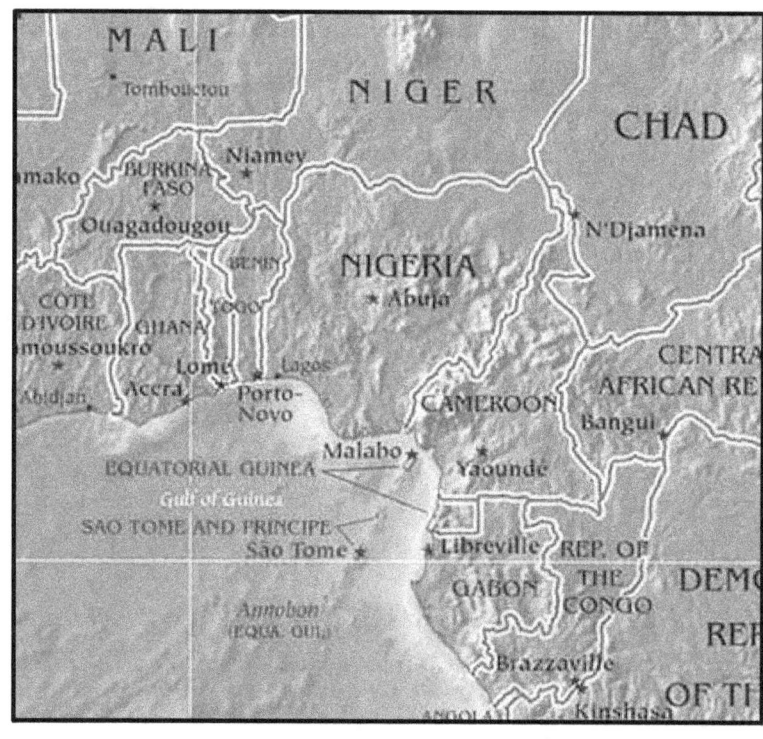

Figure 4: Nigeria 2020

In this final 2020 vignette, Nigeria is overwhelmed by growing Islamist violence.

In northern and central Nigeria, *Boko Haram* and other militant groups have taken control of most of the country and threaten the capital of Abuja. In the south, Islamist pirates have occupied large sections of the ungoverned space along the Niger River delta, and their increasing maritime attacks have brought the country's oil industry to a standstill. Over the following year, the country suffers from ever-larger mass atrocities and the displacement of over a million Christians. The chaos overwhelms the capacity of the state to address it, and the Nigerian government requests international assistance. Joined by several European allies and countries of the African Union, the Unites States deploys military forces to the southeastern coast of Nigeria as part of an international peace enforcement mission.

Joint Task Force - Nigeria (JTF-N) receives the mission to support the U.S. government's assistance effort for the Nigerian government by helping to end the violence along the Niger River delta, restore law and order, and support the return of Nigeria's oil industry to pre-conflict levels of output, under civilian control. At the direction of the U.S. ambassador, JTF-N deploys a maritime task force consisting of a reinforced Marine Expeditionary Brigade and supporting naval forces to the Niger Delta. The force is tasked to assist the Nigerian military and civil authorities by retaking three island terminals and nearby mainland installations that are critical to Nigerian oil production while also securing the waterways that run between them over a 75-mile stretch of the river. Pirate activity in the area is strong, and the force does not have a secure base from which to commence operations.

In this scenario, Marine forces must first land on the largest of the three islands and secure it as a base from which to continue subsequent operations throughout the delta. At first, the Nigerian pirates offer significant resistance using automatic weapons, rockets, and improvised explosives; but after several days, they fall back to locations on the mainland that are more secluded. The Marines then capture two island terminals and begin using them as the land-based headquarters for their subsequent operation. Naval patrol boats arrive and support the effort by conducting extensive reconnaissance and security operations along the Niger River. Supported by real-time surveillance, organic air assets, and Nigerian forces on the mainland that block the escape of the pirates, JTF-N then deploys the Marine brigade across the wide delta and onto the mainland to assault the main pirate strongholds. Over the course of the next three weeks, the Marines attack and destroy over a dozen medium-sized pirate ships, capture two small towns that served as headquarters for the pirate force, seize major weapons caches, and take several hundred prisoners. At this point, the operation assumes a more traditional peacekeeping focus, and JTF-N begins to flow food, medicine, and other supplies to the affected population. After six months, the United States returns control of the area to the government of Nigeria and the operation concludes.

U.S. participation in a stability operation of this kind would require the Joint Force to employ forcible entry by amphibious and helicopter-borne air assault to seize and hold a lodgment against armed opposition. The lodgment would then serve as a base for subsequent operations to clear a region of pirates and other armed militants. Success would require the Joint Force to achieve a level of surprise, overwhelm its opponents, and then expand the lodgment in order to set conditions for the decisive operation to clear portions of the Niger River delta and restore control to the government of Nigeria.

The critical military capabilities required to succeed in such an operation would include effective human intelligence, mobile command and control, maritime security patrols, and amphibious landing craft. The force will also require aviation-delivered fire support and a flexible logistics system that allows the operation to be sustained from the sea for a period of time extending well beyond the organic sustainment capacity of the Marine expeditionary force. In addition, the force will require clear rules of engagement (ROE) that provide the commander enough flexibility to accomplish the mission while also adhering to political, legal, operational, and diplomatic factors that may influence the mission.[20] Finally, such a force will require the ability to reinforce forward-deployed initial entry forces from the sea, deliver relief supplies to affected populations, provide for security in and among the population, and dispose of seized enemy weapons and equipment. Absent these capabilities, the U.S. may lose the ability to influence events consistent with its values and interests and may be unable to contribute effectively to regional stability in an important region of the world.

Summary

All of these operational vignettes present plausible scenarios that require the future Joint Force to conduct forcible entry operations in order to accomplish a mission. Although they differ greatly in scope and intensity, each demands that the Joint Force be able to seize and hold a lodgment against some form of armed opposition. Absent these capabilities, or lacking them in adequate scale, the Joint Force may not be able to offer policymakers feasible and acceptable options for achieving U.S. foreign policy objectives in the future, or will have to do so at an unacceptably high level of risk.

Admittedly, none of the vignettes outlined above envisions U.S. forces confronting truly great powers like Russia or China. In fact, all four vignettes foresee

---

[20] U.S. Joint Chiefs of Staff, *Joint Forcible Entry Operations,* Joint Publication 3-18 (Washington, DC: Joint Chiefs of Staff, November 27, 2012), II-10.

relatively limited conflicts against middleweight Third World opponents in regions that arguably are of less than vital strategic interest. Moreover, in all but one vignette (the Korea example), the overriding U.S. objective is merely to maintain or restore some form the *status quo ante*. However, in a situation where national survival truly is at stake in a great power conflict, U.S. policy would almost certainly seek to do much more than simply not lose the war; it would require the military to win decisively. In such a conflict, the military may require a dramatic increase in size and even greater capacity for forcible entry than described above. In addition, the Nation would be forced to recognize that prosecuting war in convenient and politically expedient ways using stand-off and precision simply will not guarantee national survival. It is in precisely such situations that the advantages of a robust forcible entry capability become most apparent. With this understanding in mind, it is now necessary to examine the current and projected forcible entry capabilities of the Joint Force and compare them to the demands of the future.

CHAPTER 4: PROJECTED CAPABILITIES AND GAPS

We are developing today the Joint Force our Nation will need in 2020. Keeping our military the best led, trained, and equipped in the world is a non-negotiable imperative. Doing so during a period of fiscal constraint will be hard. We will need to be selective in the joint capabilities we reconstitute after a decade of war. We will need to get smaller to stay strong. Importantly, we will need to be even more joint—advancing interdependence and integrating new capabilities. I am convinced we can restore versatility at an affordable cost. I am determined to build a responsive Joint Force that preserves options for our Nation.[1]

It is difficult to project today the exact size and composition of the future Joint Force. With so many political and economic variables in play, even some of the basic assumptions about resources in the Future Years Defense Program (FYDP) may be in doubt. Nevertheless, the past provides some insights about where the defense budget and its related programs are likely to head in the next seven years. The chart below depicts the historic trend for defense spending over the last 65 years. The most noticeable fact is

---

[1] Martin E. Dempsey, *Chairman's Strategic Direction to the Joint Force* (Washington, DC: U.S. Joint Chiefs of Staff, February 6, 2012), 5.

that after each of the last three major conflicts, defense spending declined by an average of 33% over the seven years that followed. In each case, a variety of unique political, economic and strategic factors combined to drive the cuts, but the pattern clearly suggests that defense spending in the next seven years is likely to decrease by a similar amount. Despite the hyperbole associated with the reductions mandated by sequestration, such cuts are actually quite consistent with historical norms. In fact, even under scenarios described by many as catastrophic, defense spending would remain at or above its long-term historic average. As Peter Singer of the Brookings Institution recently observed, even under the worst-case scenarios being discussed today, "defense spending would be reduced not to the bottom of the historic trough, but only to the rough average of overall spending."[3] The main question for purposes of this thesis is what impact these reductions will have on the ability of the Joint Force to conduct forcible entry operations.

Air and Maritime Domains

In the maritime and air domains, such reductions would probably mean the curtailment or termination of some acquisition programs, perhaps affecting major systems like the F-35. However, with DoD's current emphasis on *Air Sea Battle*, the majority of the capabilities resident in these domains are much better positioned to survive the political and economic wrangling that is to come. The 11 Carrier Strike Groups currently active in the U.S. Navy might be reduced by one or two, but an effective carrier-based force will no doubt remain a central element of U.S. maritime strategy. Amphibious ships and associated landing and support vessels will most likely face more significant cuts. Submarine forces may have to delay production of a new

---

[3] Ibid.

class of submarines, but the Navy could upgrade its existing submarine fleet and retain most, if not all, of its sub-surface force structure and capability. Anti-sub and counter-mine capabilities may even see some growth to support the operational requirements of *Air Sea Battle*, as could naval cruise missile capabilities. AEGIS ballistic missile defense systems and Submarine-based strategic nuclear forces would likewise have to be retained in full strength to retain an effective nuclear deterrent.

A significant decrement in capabilities in these areas could have serious implications for the ability of the Joint Force to secure air and sea lines of communications around the globe and in regions of strategic concern. It could also limit the ability of the Joint Force to project power rapidly to crises, and sustain that power projection over time. As prerequisites for any form of successful forcible entry operation, these capabilities must be retained. Moreover, the skillful application of maritime deterrence and power projection may even preclude the need for forcible entry in some cases; but relying on such an outcome is not a risk the nation can afford to make, even in a climate of constrained resources.

The Air Force may be forced to reduce the number of active air wings by as much as 10-15%, but will likely seek to protect as much of its combat power as possible, to include its manned fighter and bomber aircraft, as well as its aerial reconnaissance and surveillance systems.[4] Likely targets for cuts include the Intercontinental Ballistic Missile element of the nuclear triad, strategic airlift, close air support capabilities, and Air

---

[4] Systems that provide airborne surveillance are often referred to as "ISR" systems. This thesis avoids use of this term because of its imprecision and tendency to reduce reconnaissance and surveillance tasks to aerial surveillance and targeting. For further discussion, see Mark Elfendahl, "Think Beyond Targeting," *Armed Forces Journal* (February 2011), http://www. armedforcesjournal.com/2011/02/5278465/ (accessed on February 12, 2013).

Expeditionary Wings.[5] However, transport aircraft and close air support are two of the

most important capabilities in the air domain required to support forcible entry

operations. While the Air Force should not impose the sort of cuts that would place air

superiority in combat at risk, it also must never lose sight of its critical role in

transporting and supporting ground forces, especially during forcible entry.[6] Indeed,

from the standpoint of forcible entry, the greatest gap in U.S. ability to project power into

a JOA is the capacity of strategic airlift.[7] Any shortfall in air transport capability delays

the arrival of land forces and risks ceding the initiative to the enemy. Areas of likely

expansion include UAS and drones that provide overhead surveillance and attack, such as

the MQ-1 Predator and MQ-9 Reaper drones.[8]

Land Domain

If the current trajectory of defense priorities continues, reductions in spending are

likely to impact the land domain most significantly. Army and Marine Corps force

structure are among the items most often mentioned in discussions about how to cut

spending. A number of recent high-visibility proposals have suggested reducing the size

of the active Army and Marine Corps by as much as 40-50% and shifting major

capabilities into the reserve components in order to save money while protecting DoD's

---

[5] Scott Sigmund Gartner, "Sequester Offers an Opportunity to Realign National Security," *McClatchy Newspapers,* March 5, 2013, http://ebird.osd.mil/ebird2/ebfiles/e20130306917634.html (accessed March 6, 2013).

[6] Daniel Goure, "The Army Is Ready To Fight, But Can DoD Get It There?" Lexington Institute Early Warning Blog, article posted September 20, 2012, http://www. lexingtoninstitute.org/the-army-is-ready-to-fight-but-can-dod-get-it-there-?a=1 & c=1171 (accessed September 22, 2012).

[7] U.S. Army Training and Doctrine Command, *The U.S. Army Capstone Concept,* TRADOC Pam 525-3-0 (Fort Eustis, VA: U.S. Army Capabilities Integration Center, December 19, 2012), 35.

[8] To a lesser extent such expansion would also include the RQ-4 Global Hawk, RQ-7 Shadow, and RQ-11 Raven unmanned aerial systems (UAS).

ability to prosecute *Air Sea Battle*.[9] Such cuts could easily mean the loss of half the Army's airborne forces, and equally large reductions in air assault-trained infantry forces and the rotary-wing platforms that transport and support them. Combat support and sustainment forces would also have to accept substantial cuts. Further reductions in overseas basing and rotational forward deployment would only exacerbate the problem from the standpoint of access and entry, in that it could eliminate some of the more important intermediate staging bases (ISB) upon which U.S. forces have relied.

In the Marine Corps, force structure cuts of this size could easily require reducing the goal of a 2.5 MEB capability down to as little as 1.5 MEB. Such a reduction could easily mean losing the option to respond to more than one significant maritime or littoral crisis at a time with any sort of meaningful ground combat element. It would also require significant cuts to Marine air wings, including the V-22 Osprey and CH-53 Sea Stallion programs in particular. If such an approach were to prevail, the ability of the Joint Force to conduct forcible entry operations on the scale required by plausible future scenarios would be placed at a very high level of risk. As one defense expert recently observed,

> If an under-appreciation for the potential demand leads to substantial reductions in forcible entry capabilities either in the Marine Corps or in the Army, future decisionmakers' options could be greatly reduced. This also applies to careful consideration of the entire family of joint enablers that underwrite U.S. capability for forcible entry (e.g., amphibious shipping, suppression of enemy air defenses, counter-mine capabilities, and strategic and operational airlift).[10]

---

[9] For example, see Gary Roughhead and Kori Schake, *National Defense in a Time of Change* (Washington, DC: Brookings Institution, February 2013), 13, http://www.brookings.edu/~/media/research/files/papers/ 2013/02/us%20national%20defense%20changes/thp_rougheaddiscpaper.pdf (accessed on March 29, 2013). See also David W. Barno, Dr. Nora Bensahle, and Travis Sharp, "How to Cut the Defense Budget Responsibly," Center for a New American Security, http://www.cnas.org/node/7259 (accessed on March 16, 2013).

[10] Nathan Frier, *U.S. Ground Force Capabilities through 2020* (Washington DC: Center for Strategic and International Studies, October 11, 2011), 16, http://csis.org/ publication/us_ground_force_capabilities_through_2020 (accessed on October 20, 2012).

If force structure in the land domain is reduced as currently envisioned by some, the United States could probably retain the ability to gain access to key regions of the world through the use of air and maritime power, but it might not be able to do much else once it gets there. In short, it may lose the ability to fight *the other half of the battle.* When one considers that many close allies of the U.S. have already reduced their own militaries to the point where they can no longer conduct forcible entry missions independently but instead rely on the United States for this capability, the need for U.S. forces to execute forcible entry becomes all the more apparent.[11]

Even as currently organized, land component forcible entry units suffer from several significant capability gaps. First and foremost, they lack survivability, especially against hybrid adversaries and states with more capable armored forces.[12] Although air power may be effective against hardened threat ground systems, it clearly lacks the ability to occupy terrain or secure lodgments without ground forces. In addition, forcible entry units require greater mobility and firepower to operate effectively, along with moderately improved protection and fire support capabilities. Extensive analysis has shown that such improvements are the best way to improve the capabilities of entry forces in the future.[13] Without these capabilities, they risk simply impaling themselves upon their enemies the moment they arrive. What is called for is a new concept for the employment of land forces in forcible entry that avoids emerging enemy strengths while introducing greater maneuver into the force at the operational and tactical levels.

---

[11] Ibid., 14.

[12] John Matsumura et al., *Lightning over Water: Sharpening America's Light Forces for Rapid-Reaction Missions - Executive Summary* (Santa Monica, CA: RAND Arroyo Center, 2001), 1.

[13] Ibid., 25, 31.

Space and Cyber Domains

In the space and cyber domains, the future Joint Force is likely to see continued growth and expanded capabilities, particularly with respect to cyber capabilities. U.S. forces are increasingly dependent on space-based satellites for imagery, electronic intelligence, navigation and timing information, as well as global communications. In addition, a large amount of U.S. precision guided munitions and UAS rely on locational data from satellites. This reliance is likely to persist for the foreseeable future. In fact, the heavy dependence of U.S. forces on these technologies makes them a vulnerable center of gravity enemies are likely to target in the future. For at least several years, adversaries have been developing new and improved ways to use computer and electronic attacks to degrade, neutralize, or destroy U.S. command and control both in CONUS and overseas operational areas.[14] However, senior defense officials have recognized these vulnerabilities and are dedicating significant resources to protect them. In addition, there are a number of programs already underway that will use space-based and cyber capabilities to improve processing, exploitation, and dissemination (PED) of intelligence across the Joint Force.

These capabilities will be important factors in forcible entry because successful operations will most likely require greater preparation in both the space and cyber domains before entry can begin. However a number of important gaps may remain. First, entry forces still require improved communications systems that enable effective mission command on-the-move, especially from airborne platforms. Today's systems are only marginally capable of producing situational awareness en route and do not extend

---

[14] U.S. Joint Chiefs of Staff, *Joint Operational Access Concept,* Version 1.0 (Washington, DC: Joint Chiefs of Staff, January 17, 2012), 10.

connectivity to echelons below battalion level headquarters.[15] In addition, the most

capable systems typically cannot be landed or air dropped with assault forces. Improving

these capabilities will require additional time and resources to establish communications

links more quickly than is the case today. Given the right emphasis, other systems could

enable future forces to direct, if not control, activities in the space and cyber domains that

support their physical maneuver. The idea of using space and cyber capabilities to

conduct reinforcing "maneuver" in their respective domains and penetrate hostile

networks in support of physical maneuver in the land, sea and air domains is clearly

articulated in the *JOAC*, but will only achieve the desired effect if properly resourced.[16]

Before the US is forced to compete seriously in either of these domains, it should

develop more effective offensive cyber capabilities that will enable US forces to inflict

chaos on enemy systems while protecting friendly systems. In addition, the United States

should not shy away from the notion of "weaponizing" outer space. The US still has an

enormous advantage in this area, and such steps may serve to extend that dominance for

many years to come.

Special Operations

Perhaps the only major areas of defense capability related to forcible entry that

will not be significantly impacted by current defense priorities are those related to SOF.

Current military strategy states that U.S. forces will continue to expand and improve the

capabilities of SOF and will continue to rely on them for a wide variety of missions and

---

[15] Jason G. Rakocy and Robert Kruger, Jr., *Joint Forcible Entry Warfighter Experiment (JFEWE) 2011 Final Report* (Fort Benning, GA: U.S. Army Maneuver Battle Lab, 2011), Appendix F, Tab B, 8-9.
[16] *JOAC*, 31.

requirements.[17] SOF capabilities are expected to grow over the next seven years and will be an essential part of U.S. efforts to shape the security environment through engagement, training and advisory missions, and foreign internal defense (FID). More directly related to forcible entry, SOF will continue to command an impressive capability for direct action missions, strategic raids, and counterterrorism operations. While these operations may constitute a form of forcible entry, their scale will continue to be relatively small. In support of larger forcible entry operations by conventional forces, SOF will continue to provide important functions such as special reconnaissance and strategic targeting using joint fires.

In larger scale operations, such as the Pakistan vignette in Chapter 3, SOF may require substantial augmentation by conventional forces. In this event, the largest potential gap is in training. If conventional forces and SOF do not put in place now the necessary forcing mechanisms to drive them toward greater interoperability and mutual support, they are likely to revert back to their respective institutional "default settings" and lose much of the collaboration and interoperability they now enjoy. In addition, they may lack the necessary training to execute certain operations quickly. However, proper emphasis by senior leaders will go a long way toward precluding such an outcome.

Summary

Current defense priorities and projected resources are likely to account for many of the more important requirements for future forcible entry. However, without some important adjustments, these priorities are likely to produce a number of gaps the Joint

---

[17] U.S. Joint Chiefs of Staff, *The National Military Strategy of the United States of America 2011: Redefining America's Military Leadership* (Washington, DC: U.S. Joint Chiefs of Staff, February 8, 2011), 19.

Force must close if it expects to conduct successful forcible entry in the future. Perhaps the most notable of these is the lack of recognition that forcible entry is still a requirement. As recently as several years ago, retired Army General Carl Stiner observed that there has been no mention of forcible entry in any QDR documents since 2001. The last mention of forcible entry as a required capability in the Joint Strategic Capabilities Plan (JSCP) was in 2002. Until very recently, the Global Response Force (GRF) execute order made no mention of forcible entry capability, training or exercises, and there was no comprehensive statement of requirements in any DoD documents.[18]

With so much emphasis in recent years on *Air Sea Battle*, much of the intellectual energy related to future defense capabilities has focused on questions of access, lines of communications, and getting to the fight as opposed to actually fighting on foreign soil. In this context, it is instructive to note that the Joint Staff's own *Decade of War* study does not contain a single reference to any form of forcible entry.[19] This absence only underscores the fact that the Joint Force has learned next to nothing about forcible entry over the last decade. On the contrary, it has forgotten some of the more important things it used to know. After almost 12 years of irregular conflict and extended commitments overseas, many defense analysts believe they now know what the new American way of war ought to be. However, the force reductions now underway are already changing that style of fighting in important ways, and in a few years, they are likely to create a different set of shortcomings than those the Joint Force had to overcome only recently.[20]

---

[18] Carl Stiner and Daniel R. Schroeder, "The Army and Joint Forcible Entry," *Army* 59, no. 11 (November 2009): 19.

[19] U.S. Joint Chiefs of Staff, *Decade of War, Volume 1: Enduring Lessons from the Past Decade of Operations* (Suffolk, VA: Joint Center for Operational Analysis, June 15, 2012), 2.

[20] Antulio J. Echevarria, II, "What Is Wrong with the American Way of War?" *Prism* 3, no. 4 (September 2012): 114.

CHAPTER 5: RECOMMENDATIONS

> Operations Golden Pheasant, Urgent Fury, Just Cause, Desert Storm, Uphold Democracy, Enduring Freedom and Iraqi Freedom have served as evidence of the continuing need to include joint forcible entry operations in our guidance, doctrine, training and planning. No one can anticipate where the nation may have to respond again, but a trained and demonstrated joint forcible entry capability is too important a matter of national security to ignore.[1]

To ensure the Joint Force of 2020 has the ability to conduct successful forcible entry operations in support of national strategy, DoD will have to adjust its current trajectory and place greater priority on developing and maintaining the right capabilities and forces. In support of this outcome, the chapter that follows provides five specific recommendations for improving the ability of the Joint Force to conduct forcible entry.

Retain Air and Maritime Superiority

Among the most important prerequisites for successful forcible entry operations are air and maritime superiority.[2] They set the conditions for successful entry, and without them, any forcible entry operation would be exceptionally risky. The recently published reports that guided development of the *Air Sea Battle* concept emphasize the importance of these capabilities not simply as ways to assure access, but also as effective deterrents to potential opponents like China or Iran.[3] However, the authors of the concept suggest that the era of uncontested U.S. dominance of the air and sea may be approaching

---

[1] Carl Stiner and Daniel R. Schroeder, "The Army and Joint Forcible Entry," *Army* 59, no. 11 (November 2009): 20.

[2] U.S. Joint Chiefs of Staff, *Joint Forcible Entry Operations,* Joint Publication 3-18 (Washington, DC: Joint Chiefs of Staff, November 27, 2012), III-4.

[3] Jan van Tol et al., *AirSea Battle: A Point of Departure Operational Concept* (Washington, DC: Center for Strategic and Budgetary Assessments, 2010), 40.

an end.[4] They further acknowledge that *Air Sea Battle* by itself is not a war-winning concept, but rather a way to help set conditions at the operational level while deterring unfavorable competition in the air and maritime domains.[5] Accordingly, the concept advocates strengthening America's air and naval capabilities while also adopting new cost-imposing strategies such as improved air and missile defense, cyber-electronic warfare, and improved sub-surface warfare capabilities. In addition, the concept recognizes that air superiority likewise makes a major contribution to effective anti-submarine warfare.[6]

To maintain air and maritime superiority, the Joint Force must continue to develop capable 5th generation combat aircraft capable of defeating any potential enemy as well as improved reconnaissance and surveillance systems. In addition, air and maritime superiority require improved missile, missile defense, and submarine forces. All of these capabilities are important to a successful forcible entry operation, but perhaps most important is the ability to employ effective joint fires in support of arriving land forces. Accordingly, programs such as the F-35 and the development of improved missiles should continue, but only at levels required to attain and maintain air superiority, while also ensuring essential air support to forcible entry missions.

Closely related to retaining air superiority is the requirement to maintain a force of fixed and rotary-wing transport aircraft that can move the necessary combat power quickly enough to seize, retain, and exploit the initiative on land. Under the current defense program, resources for strategic and theater lift are expected to drop significantly, but this situation must be corrected if future forcible entry missions are to succeed. The

---

[4] Ibid., 26-27.
[5] Ibid., ix.
[6] Ibid., 69.

number of C-17 and C-130 aircraft must be adequate to support the movement of a full brigade of airborne forces at once, along with all enablers. In addition, the Services should retain enough V-22 Osprey and CH-53 Sea Stallion helicopters to insert at least two battalions of troops into two separate theaters simultaneously. Finally, DoD should pursue development of a Joint Future Theater Lift aircraft that can take off and land vertically on unimproved or improvised fields.[7] Such a capability would expand by an order of magnitude the number of locations where U.S. forces could land while also enabling joint commanders to employ them at positions of greatest tactical and operational advantage rather than in places where infrastructure may be much better defended.

Create Air-Deployable Strike Forces

The most significant change the future Joint Force should make with respect to forcible entry capability is to organize and equip its entry forces with the mobility and firepower necessary to survive and succeed in the future operational environment. Today's Army and Marine forces assigned to forcible entry missions are simply not robust enough to defeat capable opponents and the hybrid threats emerging around the world. Without additional mobility and firepower, and at least moderate protection, these entry forces may simply impale themselves on more-capable enemies rather than defeat them. Because future ground contingencies may emerge with little to no strategic warning, the Joint Force needs entry forces with greater combat power that can deploy

---

[7] Patrick J. Donahue and Frank Womble, "Getting there is Half the Battle: How to Fix Ground Force Mobility," *Armed Forces Journal* (October 2011), http://www.armedforcesjournal.com/2011/10/7613 840/ (accessed November 9, 2012).

from strategic distances and operate effectively against capable threats in A2/AD environments.[8]

There have been a number of proposals in recent years to create such forces. Until the mid-1990s, the Army's Armored Gun System (AGS) program was intended to meet this requirement in part, but Army leaders cancelled it to save money. In 2000, retired brigadier generals David Grange and Huba Wass de Czege proposed a concept called *Air-Mech Strike*.[9] Their idea, adapted later by others, was to create air-deployable mechanized forces that could fight immediately upon delivery to shock enemies and enable the Joint Force to bypass the requirement to build combat power over time.[10] More recently, others have argued that Army Stryker or Marine LAV units could be air-dropped to provide a similar capability.[11] However, neither the Stryker nor the LAV is truly a fighting vehicle, and both lack the cross-country mobility and firepower needed to defeat capable opponents and hybrid threats.

A far more promising approach would be to reconfigure the Army's airborne formations and create four brigades of all-arms light mechanized strike forces that could be delivered by either air or sea. Such forces could conduct forcible entry as part of the Global Response Force then expand an airhead or landing zone by striking out rapidly to

---

[8] Nathan Frier, *U.S. Ground Force Capabilities through 2020* (Washington DC: Center for Strategic and International Studies, October 11, 2011), 15, http://csis.org/ publication/us_ground_force_capabilities_ through_2020 (accessed on October 20, 2012).

[9] David L. Grange et al., *Air-Mech-Strike: Asymmetrical Maneuver Warfare for the 21st Century* (Paducah, KY: Turner Publications, 2002), 1-4.

[10] Timothy M. Gilhool, "Pegasus Unbound? The Challenge of Sustainment and Endurance in Airborne Joint Forcible Entry Operations" (Fort Leavenworth, KS: U.S. Army Command and General Staff College School of Advanced Military Studies, May, 26, 2005), 52-53. In Defense Technical Information Center, http://www.dtic.mil/cgi-bin/GetTRDoc?AD =ADA437595 (accessed September 13, 2012).

[11] Mark G. Czelusta, "Global Strike Task Force and Stryker Brigade Combat Team: Prospects for Integration in the Forcible Entry Mission," (Fort Leavenworth, KS: U.S. Army Command and General Staff College, June 6, 2003), 62. In Defense Technical Information Center, http://www.dtic mil/dtic/tr/ fulltext/u2/a416072 .pdf (accessed September 13, 2012).

seize key terrain and conduct reconnaissance ahead of follow-on forces.[12] In addition,

they could block reacting enemy forces and buy time for the JFC to develop the situation

while additional combat power arrives. Supported by the right joint enablers, such forces

could vastly improve the ability of the Joint Force to execute forcible entry. The

principal combat vehicles of such units would need to be similar in capabilities to the

former AGS, but updated with current technologies. Among current combat vehicles, the

German Puma and Russian BMD-4 may represent the best off-the-shelf options, and they

could be acquired quickly. Without some form of light armored capability, future forcible

entry operations will pose increased risks to the assault force, result in greater casualties,

and perhaps even risk mission failure.[13]

In addition to reorganizing its entry forces, the future Joint Force must also

employ them more effectively. One way to accomplish this is to project them into

austere and unexpected penetration points and landing zones, rather than ports or

airfields, in order to bypass established defenses and attack enemy vulnerabilities

indirectly.[14] To seize, retain, and exploit the initiative against future threats, joint

commanders will need to conduct multiple forms of forcible entry simultaneously, while

synchronizing airborne, air assault, and amphibious operations in mutually supporting

ways. By operating in this manner, they will present enemies with a variety of tactical

and operational dilemmas, throw them off balance, and destroy their will to fight.

---

[12] Douglas A. Macgregor, *Breaking the Phalanx: A New Design for Landpower in the 21st Century* (Westport, CT: Praeger, 1997), 79-80.

[13] Bill Hix and Mark C. Smith, "Armor's Asymmetric Advantage: Why a Smaller Army Needs Mobile Protected Firepower" *Armed Forces Journal* (October 2012), http://www.armedforcesjournal.com/2012/10/11460231/ (accessed February 24, 2013).

[14] U.S. Army Training and Doctrine Command and U.S. Marine Corps Combat Development Command, *Gaining and Maintaining Access: An Army-Marine Corps Concept* (Fort Eustis and Quantico, VA: U.S. Army Capabilities Integration Center and U.S. Marine Corps Combat Development Command, March 2012), 7.

Historically, the complementary employment of airborne and amphibious forces has always been the most effective way to project power.[15] In the future, it will also be one of the most important ways to overcome enemy A2/AD capabilities and achieve the level of cross-domain synergy envisioned in current joint concepts.[16]

Future entry forces will also need to use mobility and dispersion to avoid presenting the enemy lucrative targets. In response to the advent of new and more lethal weapons, battlefields have been emptying over the last 50 years as forces have dispersed to avoid destruction.[17] By applying the concept of "dispersed mobile warfare" to entry operations, JFCs could significantly mitigate the impact of enemy precision-guided munitions while using the improved mobility of joint entry forces to maneuver against enemy vulnerabilities rather than react to enemy strengths.[18] Ultimately, the forces that enter an operational area will have to transition more rapidly from entry to offensive operations and be able to sustain that effort until additional forces arrive.[19]

Develop Effective UAS and Counter-UAS Systems

Among the many emerging technologies that may impact future forcible entry operations, unmanned aerial systems (UAS) offer significant potential. Employed properly, they could provide U.S. forces immediate situational awareness of conditions on the ground at the point of entry and the surrounding areas. To ensure the effectiveness

---

[15] Sean P. Kelly, "Airborne Assault Forces: The Most Expedient and Practical Forcible Entry Response Available in Today's Contemporary Operating Environment" (Newport, RI: Naval War College, May 4, 2012), 17. In Defense Technical Information Center, http://www.dtic mil/cgi-bin/GetTRDoc?AD=ADA56 3877&Location=U2&doc=GetTRDoc.pdf (accessed October 22, 2012).

[16] U.S. Joint Chiefs of Staff, *Joint Operational Access Concept,* Version 1.0 (Washington, DC: Joint Chiefs of Staff, January 17, 2012), 14.

[17] Douglas A. Macgregor, "Thoughts on Force Design in an Era of Shrinking Defense Budgets." *Joint Force Quarterly* 63, (October 2011): 26.

[18] Ibid., 23-24.

[19] U.S. Army Training and Doctrine Command, *The U.S. Army Capstone Concept,* TRADOC Pam 525-3-0 (Fort Eustis, VA: U.S. Army Capabilities Integration Center, December 19, 2012), 15.

of future operations, the Joint Force should develop a robust tactical UAS capability that can be airdropped or landed ashore with assault forces in sufficient quantities to enable commanders to achieve situational awareness as rapidly as possible.[20] These systems should also be capable of being armed, such that they can provide a form of immediate fire support to entry forces and combine their capabilities with those of traditional fixed-wing air support.[21] Such a capability is particularly important given the expansion of threat capabilities in precision-guided munitions. U.S. forces will need this capability as soon as they land in order to preclude or mitigate intended enemy actions to retain the initiative. The development of joint tactics and doctrine for the use of UAS should also be a priority for the Joint Force.[22]

In addition, the U.S. military should develop a more effective counter-UAS capability and tactics. Between now and 2020, small airborne systems will continue to proliferate rapidly among likely adversaries, especially those who cannot compete with the U.S. in major combat aircraft due to their high cost. Hybrid adversaries in particular may seek to use swarms of small, relatively inexpensive UAS to attack U.S. forces and limit the effectiveness of friendly drones. The Joint Force should anticipate this development now and develop systems that can neutralize threat UAS over and near

---

[20] Jason G. Rakocy and Robert Kruger, Jr., *Joint Forcible Entry Warfighter Experiment (JFEWE) 2011 Final Report* (Fort Benning, GA: U.S. Army Maneuver Battle Lab, 2011), Appendix F, Tab A, 5. The purpose of this major joint experiment was to examine the ability of the Joint Force to conduct forcible entry operations by parachute, air, amphibious, or land assault into austere locations, overcome or avoid enemy anti-access and area denial efforts, and present the enemy with multiple threats from unexpected locations in order to revise concepts and inform DOTMLPF solutions across warfighting functions.

[21] Steven W. Gilland, "Forcible Entry Contingency Operations: Effective Employment of Tactical Aerospace Power in Support of the Joint Task Force Commander" (Maxwell Air Force Base, AL: Air University, March 2002), 26. In Defense Technical Information Center, http://www.dtic mil/dtic/tr/fulltext/u2/a420442 .pdf (accessed September 13, 2012).

[22] *JFEWE 2011 Final Report*, Appendix F, Tab E, 7.

planned lodgments. An effective counter-UAS capability should also be capable of being put into operation very soon after an assault force has landed.[23]

Improve Sea-Based Logistics Capability

Another key enabler of future joint forcible entry operations is an effective sea-based logistics system that can provide a continuous flow of sustainment to forces ashore for short durations or extended periods. With the growing likelihood that forward air and sea ports of debarkation (APODs and SPODs) may be unavailable to U.S. forces, the future Joint Force must anticipate such situations and compensate for them by improving its ability to sustain forces directly from the sea.

Two mutually-supporting approaches worthy of implementation are the concepts of Joint Seabasing and Joint Logistics Over-The-Shore (JLOTS). Joint Seabasing envisions assembling and employing a mix of strategic and theater seaborne assets to direct, employ, protect, and sustain joint forces in a way that avoids many emerging threat A2/AD capabilities.[24] JLOTS supports Joint Seabasing by providing the logistics assets necessary to sustain joint forces from the sea in situations where critical nodes such APODs and SPODs are unavailable.[25] JLOTS operations can also provide the ability to sustain forces in austere areas or where port facilities are damaged or inadequate. In addition, JLOTS could provide a means of intra-theater sealift to move forces, equipment, and sustainment cargo closer to places of employment.

---

[23] Ibid., Appendix F, Tab A, 17.

[24] U.S. Navy Fleet Forces Command, *Concept for Employment of Current Seabasing Capabilities: Integrating Seabasing Capabilities Into Exercises and Experiments* (Norfolk, VA: U.S. Fleet Forces Command, June 29, 2010), 5.

[25] U.S. Joint Chiefs of Staff, *Joint Logistics Over-The-Shore,* Joint Publication 4-01.6 (Washington, DC: U.S. Joint Chiefs of Staff, November 27, 2012), I-2.

Among the many outcomes of the 2011 Joint Forcible Entry Warfighting Experiment (JFEWE) was the finding that a mobile system of sea-based joint platforms could provide an invaluable operational and sustainment capability in support of forcible entry operations.[26] Such a system could allow JFCs much greater latitude to select and conduct operations in ways that turn or envelop enemy forces, seize key terrain and facilities, disrupt enemy rear areas, or clear littorals of forces with A2/AD capabilities.[27] In addition, the use of Joint Seabasing and JLOTS could allow the Joint Force to redirect its effort from one area of conflict to another much more rapidly than is currently the case--a significant consideration in an era of constrained resources where strategy demands such agility.[28] From a sustainment perspective, these concepts could not only reduce overall demand, but also minimize the operational pause typically imposed on JFCs during the build-up of large stockpiles.[29] Moreover, such an approach could reduce the demand for strategic airlift and provide the Joint Force a more flexible way of sustaining the force over shorter ground lines of communications.

Retain Sufficient Forcible Entry Force Structure

The Joint Force of 2020 must retain enough force structure capable of forcible entry to provide policymakers with options for entry by any means. Accordingly, the Army should retain a total of four airborne BCTs in its active component force structure while reconfiguring them as light mechanized strike groups. Three of these BCTs would rotate responsibility as the airborne element of the Global Response Force (GRF). The

---

[26] *JFEWE 2011 Final Report*, Appendix F, Tab C, 7.

[27] Ibid., Appendix F, Tab B, 11.

[28] Christopher L. Sutherland, "Joint Seabasing and Joint Vision 2020" (Quantico, VA: U.S. Marine Corps Command and Staff College, Marine Corps University, April 24, 2009), 13. In Defense Technical Information Center, http://oai.dtic mil/oai/oai?verb=getRecord&metadataPrefix=html&identifier=ADA510 839 (accessed October 22, 2012).

[29] *JFEWE 2011 Final Report,* Appendix F, Tab C, 2.

fourth would provide a strategic reserve for contingencies elsewhere around the globe and serve as a force of first resort in a secondary theater. In addition, the Army should retain three IBCTs highly trained in air assault operations with access to enough assault and attack helicopter assets to conduct a brigade-sized air assault operation. The three IBCTs would rotate in readiness such that, at any given time, one of them would be ready for immediate employment around the world.

The Navy and Marine Corps should maintain a 2.0 MEB capability in order to provide the option for rapid-reaction amphibious operations in two separate theaters, while retaining the ability to employ both MEBs simultaneously in a single theater if required. Each MEB should have a light mechanized capability to provide greater mobility and firepower to the infantry. Such a force would also include the requisite air wings and logistics packages of the Air Combat Element (ACE) and Logistics Combat Element (LCE). The Navy should support this requirement with enough upgraded amphibious ships, docking capability, and landing craft to enable the simultaneous employment of both MEBs. In addition, Marine Forces should maintain at least 12 squadrons of V-22 Osprey helicopters, with six focused on the Pacific and six on the Atlantic, along with enough CH-53 assets to move a regiment of infantry from a sea-based platform or intermediate staging base on land to the place of employment.

The Air Force should continue to procure enough fourth and fifth generation combat aircraft to ensure air superiority and effective strike capability in any forcible entry scenario. Of the four scenarios cited in this paper, the most resource intensive would clearly be the Iran and Korea scenarios. The Air Force must also ensure it has the necessary aerial surveillance assets to provide situational understanding to operational

64

commanders and tactical forces. To move and employ the Army's airborne forces, the Air Force must also maintain enough strategic lift capacity to transport and airdrop an entire airborne BCT in a single operation, with assets left over to maintain steady-state airlift requirements elsewhere around the world.

The Navy should maintain a 1.0 CSG capability at all times in both the Pacific and Atlantic in order to deter would-be aggressors, ensure access to key strategic regions, provide immediate strike capabilities, and secure sea lines of communication. With at least eight CSGs in the fleet, the Navy could surge this capability to 2.0 in both oceans for significant periods in response to operational requirements. Upon their employment, naval forces must be able to achieve maritime supremacy quickly, with the ability to reapportion assets between two major contingencies as required. In addition, naval air power would combine with that of the Air Force and Marines to provide adequate air interdiction and close air support to arriving entry forces.

Finally, the Joint Force of 2020 must sustain the capabilities of its Special Operations units to conduct strategic raids, direct action, counterterrorism and other specialized missions around the world. Critical force structure to retain includes the Army's 75th Infantry (Ranger) Regiment, the 160th Special Operations Aviation Regiment, the Navy's Sea Air Land (SEAL) teams, and other national assets dedicated to the ongoing counterterrorism effort. As the vignettes in this thesis suggest, the Nation requires enough SOF to distribute them for a variety of sustained, low-level operations all around the world, but also enough to concentrate them if required in larger operations, such as entry operations to secure WMD or defeat aggression.

In a shrinking military, any discussion of force structure to protect must also consider the trade-offs necessary to protect it. In this regard, the Army could inactivate several more of its Stryker or Infantry brigades, along with their associated supporting units. The Army could also reduce the size of its reserve components, an option that has received virtually no mention to date. The Air Force should cut the size of its nuclear missile and bomber forces as part of an overall reshaping of the Nation's nuclear triad. In addition, cutting the F-35 program in half and reducing the number of air wings would provide a significant portion of the force structure and acquisition dollars necessary to organize and equip more capable entry forces in the Army and Marine Corps. The Navy could reduce the number of its aircraft carriers and their associated air wings while still ensuring a more than capable strike capability in two oceans. Finally, the number of joint commands could be reduced significantly, saving a considerable number of billets and substantial resources. Instead of making new commands like U.S. Cyber Command, DoD should reduce the number of unified commands while recognizing with candor that it is heavily over-invested in strategic intelligence organizations. By consolidating a number of these, the department could cut thousands of unneeded positions, save considerable resources, and begin to rationalize the massive intelligence bureaucracy that currently exists in Washington and around the country. Naturally, any decisions related to these kinds of force structure trade-offs would require careful analysis of costs and benefits, but such a detailed effort is beyond the scope of this thesis.

CHAPTER 6: CONCLUSION

And you shall hear of wars and rumors of wars. See that ye be not troubled. For these things must come to pass, but the end is not yet. For yet shall nation rise against nation, and kingdom against kingdom.

– Gospel of St. Matthew[1]

Over the next decade, a rapidly changing operational environment will present the United States with a number of important strategic challenges. An essential element of the response to these challenges will be the ability to project military power into strategically important regions of the world in order to deter or defeat aggression. Faced with a variety of new threats and tactics, a contracting global force posture, and considerable pressure to reduce defense spending, the U.S. military must significantly improve its ability to conduct effective forcible entry operations in order to meet the requirements of national strategy.

This thesis has suggested a number of steps the U.S. military should take to ensure the Joint Force of 2020 retains the ability to conduct successful forcible entry. The most critical prerequisite for this capability is the maintenance of air and maritime superiority over increasingly capable potential opponents. However, the military cannot stop only halfway into the fight. It also requires rapidly deployable ground strike forces that can respond from strategic distances to any potential crisis by placing combat power into areas of vital strategic interest to the United States. Ideally, these forces should be air-deployable and possess enough mobility and firepower to maneuver, fight, and win upon arrival against capable enemies in distant theaters of operations. These lightly armored strike forces require a new concept for employment that avoids enemy strengths

---

[1] Matt. 24:6-7 (Douay-Rheims New Testament, 1899 American Edition).

and leverages cross-domain synergy. Understanding new technologies will also be critical. For this reason, the U.S. military should invest in expanded UAS and counter-UAS capabilities that provide improved situational awareness and new ways to employ joint fires to help ground forces seize, retain and exploit the initiative. The future will also require new approaches to sustainment. Accordingly, the military should pursue sea-based logistics concepts that allow it to bypass or avoid the area denial tactics of capable opponents. Finally, the U.S. military must ensure that it retains sufficient force structure capable of forcible entry in the active component, such that it can respond immediately with trained and ready forces whenever required. An over-reliance on stand-off weapons or precision engagements as a principal way to fight future wars is not likely to be enough to defend and advance American interests in a chaotic and violent world.

As politicians and defense officials consider how to shape the military of the post-Afghanistan era, they would be well advised to sustain a robust forcible entry capability across the Joint Force. Without it, the military may be unable to offer options to the president and Secretary of Defense at an acceptable level of risk when faced with crises or conflicts that may emerge. As retired Army General Carl Stiner recently observed, "It doesn't matter what the situation, if you can't force your way into an area and put boots on the ground to take control, you're not going to change anything. Without an effective forcible entry capability, the U.S. military simply won't be relevant."[2] All of the Services have an important role to play in joint forcible entry, and such operations are not likely to succeed unless the capabilities resident in all domains are combined as part of a joint effort. Such an outcome requires focus from the top down to ensure priorities

---

[2] Carl Stiner, "Operation Just Cause" (lecture, Joint Forces Staff College, Norfolk, VA, March 26, 2013).

and resources are applied properly. It also requires the military to make necessary trade-offs and accept a greater level of risk in a number of other important capabilities.

Shortly before assuming command of U.S. Central Command, Marine General James Mattis remarked, "When the U.S.A. loses the ability to forcibly enter another's terrain, we've surrendered our influence in a world where that surrender won't play well."[3] Despite the obvious wisdom of this statement, forcible entry is not frequently discussed in many strategy and policy circles. Instead of thinking critically about what is required to seize, retain, and exploit the initiative against adaptive and increasingly capable adversaries, some analysts apparently believe a strategy focused on access and "deterrence by denial" will be adequate to defend the country and advance U.S. interests in a dangerous world. The lack of discussion might tempt one to believe that "putting your young men into the mud" is something that, once again, will never reoccur.[4] However, the United States has not seen its last war; and when military conflict comes again--at a time and place we least expect--America will have to make a choice about whether to fight, and how. In his classic history of the Korean War, T.R. Fehrenbach described America's unpreparedness for the conflict that erupted suddenly in the middle of the last century. As he observed, any military force that is unprepared to fight in ways required for victory will eventually be defeated by a more capable, more resilient, or craftier enemy.[5] For Fehrenbach, the lesson of Korea was that it happened. If that is true, then the lesson for America with respect to forcible entry is that it will happen again.

---

[3] James N. Mattis, as quoted in "Joint Forcible Entry," Powerpoint presentation by Lieutenant General Frank G. Helmick at the U.S. Army Infantry Warfighter Forum, Fort Benning, GA, September 15, 2010, http://www.benning.army.mil/iwc/2010/Downloads/LTGHelmick.ppt (accessed March 16, 2013).

[4] T.R. Fehrenbach, *This Kind of War: A Study in Unpreparedness* (New York, NY: MacMillan, 1963), 427.

[5] Ibid., 656.

GLOSSARY

KEY MILITARY TERMS:

Air Assault Operation: An operation in which assault forces use the mobility of rotary-wing assets to maneuver under the control of a ground or air maneuver commander to engage enemy forces or to seize and hold key terrain. (JP 3-18)

Airborne Operation: An operation involving the air movement into an objective area of combat forces and their logistic support for execution of a tactical, operational, or strategic mission. (JP 3-18)

Amphibious Operation: An operation launched from the sea by an amphibious force, embarked in ships or craft with the primary purpose of introducing a landing force ashore to accomplish the assigned mission. (JP 3-02)

Anti-Access: Those actions and capabilities, usually long-range, designed to prevent an opposing force from entering an operational area. (JOAC)

Area Denial: Those actions and capabilities, usually of shorter range, designed to limit an opposing force's freedom of action within an operational area. (JOAC)

Forcible Entry: Seizing and holding of a military lodgment in the face of armed opposition. (JP 3-18)

Joint Operations Area: An area of land, sea, and airspace, defined by a geographic combatant commander or subordinate unified commander, in which a joint force commander (normally a joint task force commander) conducts military operations to accomplish a specific mission. (JP 3-0)

Line of Communications: A route, either land, water, and/or air, that connects an operating military force with a base of operations and along which supplies and military forces move. (JP 1-02)

Lodgment: A designated area in a hostile or potentially hostile operational area that, when seized and held, makes the continuous landing of troops and materiel possible and provides maneuver space for subsequent operations (JP 3-18)

Operational Area: An overarching term encompassing more descriptive terms for geographic areas in which military operations are conducted. Operational areas include, but are not limited to, such descriptors as: area of responsibility, theater of war, theater of operations, joint operations area, amphibious objective area, joint special operations area, and area of operations. (JP 3-0)

FREQUENTLY USED ABBREVIATIONS:

A2/AD: Anti-Access and Area Denial
ABN: Airborne
ACE: Air Combat Element
APOD: Aerial Port of Debarkation
ARG: Amphibious Ready Group
BCT: Brigade Combat Team
BMD: Ballistic Missile Defense
CAS: Close Air Support
CCDR: Combatant Commander
CCJO: Capstone Concept for Joint Operations
CJTF: Combined Joint Task Force
CONUS: Continental United States
CSG: Carrier Strike Group
DoD: Department of Defense
ESG: Expeditionary Strike Group
IADS: Integrated Air Defense System
IC: Intelligence Community
ICBM: Intercontinental Ballistic Missile
JFACC: Joint Force Air Component Commander
JFC: Joint Force Commander
JFEO: Joint Forcible Entry Operations
JFLCC: Joint Force Land Component Commander
JFMCC: Joint Force Maritime Component Commander
JFSOCC: Joint Force Special Operations Component Commander
JFEWE: Joint Forcible Entry Warfighter Experiment
JLOTS: Joint Logistics Over-The-Shore
JOAC: Joint Operational Access Concept
JOE: Joint Operating Environment
LCE: Logistics Combat Element
LOC: Line of Communications
MBL: Maneuver Battle Lab
MCoE: Maneuver Center of Excellence
MCWL: Marine Corps Warfighting Lab
MEB: Marine Expeditionary Brigade
NEO: Noncombatant Evacuation Operations
NMS: National Military Strategy
OE: Operational Environment
OPLAN: Operation Plan
SAM: Surface to Air Missile
SOF: Special Operations Forces
SPOD: Sea Port of Debarkation
SSBN: Ballistic Missile Submarine
TBM: Tactical Ballistic Missile
UAS: Unmanned Aerial System

BIBLIOGRAPHY

Appleman, Roy E. *South to the Naktong, North to the Yalu: The United States Army in the Korean War.* Washington, DC: Office of the Chief of Military History, Department of the Army, 1961.

Barno, David W., Nora Bensahle, and Travis Sharp. "How to Cut the Defense Budget Responsibly." Center for a New American Security. http://www.cnas.org/node/7259 (accessed March 16, 2013).

Bennett, Michael C. "U.S. Special Operations Forces." Lecture, Joint Forces Staff College, September 14, 2012.

Buchanan, Jeffrey, Maxie Y. Davis, and Lee T. Wight. "Death of the Combatant Command? Toward a Joint Interagency Approach." *Joint Force Quarterly* 52 (January 2009): 92-96. http://www.ndu.edu/press/lib/pdf/jfq-52/JFQ-52.pdf (accessed February 18, 2013).

Button, Robert, Irv Blickstein, John Gordon, Peter Wilson, and Jessie Riposo. *A Preliminary Investigation of Ship Acquisition Options for Joint Forcible Entry Operations.* Arlington, VA: RAND National Defense Research Institute, May 16, 2005. http://www.rand.org/content/dam/rand/pubs/monographs/2005/RAND_MG179.pdf (accessed February 23, 2013).

Corbett, Julian S. *Principles of Maritime Strategy.* Mineola, NY: Dover Publications, 2004.

Czelusta, Mark G. "Global Strike Task Force and Stryker Brigade Combat Team: Prospects for Integration in the Forcible Entry Mission." Fort Leavenworth, KS: U.S. Army Command and General Staff College, June 6, 2003. In Defense Technical Information Center, http://www.dtic. mil/dtic/tr/fulltext/u2/a416072.pdf (accessed September 13, 20120).

Dempsey, Martin E. *Chairman's Strategic Direction to the Joint Force.* Washington, DC: U.S. Joint Chiefs of Staff, February 6, 2012.

Dick, C. J. *The Future of Conflict: Looking Out to 2020.* Camberley, UK: Conflict Studies Research Center, 2003.

Donahue, Patrick J. and Frank Womble. "Getting there is Half the Battle: How to Fix Ground Force Mobility." *Armed Forces Journal* (October 2011). http://www.armedforcesjournal.com/2011/10/7613840/ (accessed November 9, 2012).

Echevarria, Antulio J., II. "What Is Wrong with the American Way of War?" *Prism* 3, no. 4 (September 2012): 109-115. .

———. "Rethinking the American Way of War and the Role of Landpower." U.S. Army War College Strategic Studies Institute, article posted September 10, 2012. http://www.strategicstudiesinstitute.army.mil/index.cfm/ articles/Rethinking-the-American-Way-of-War-and-the-Role-of-Landpower/2012/09/10 (accessed September 25, 2012)

Elfendahl, Mark. "Think Beyond Targeting." *Armed Forces Journal* (February 2011). http://www.armedforcesjournal.com/2011/02/5278465/ (accessed February 12, 2013).

Fehrenbach, T.R. *This Kind of War: A Study in Unpreparedness*. New York, NY: MacMillan, 1963.

Freier, Nathan. *U.S. Ground Force Capabilities through 2020*. Washington, DC: Center for Strategic and International Studies, October 11, 2011. http://csis.org/publication/us_ ground_force_capabilities_through_2020 (accessed October 20, 2012).

Gehris, Scott A. "Forcible Entry from the Sea: Operational Commanders Tools and Techniques for Execution in Today's Environment." Newport, RI: Naval War College, May 4, 2009. In Defense Technical Information Center, http://www.dtic.mil/cgi-bin/GetTRDoc?AD=ADA502970&Location=U2&doc=GetTRDoc.pdf (accessed September 13, 2012).

Gilhool, Timothy M. "Pegasus Unbound? The Challenge of Sustainment and Endurance in Airborne Joint Forcible Entry Operations." Fort Leavenworth, KS: U.S. Army Command and General Staff College School of Advanced Military Studies, May 26, 2005. In Defense Technical Information Center, http://www.dtic.mil/cgi-bin/GetTRDoc?AD=ADA437595 (accessed September 13, 2012).

Gilland, Steven W. "Forcible Entry Contingency Operations: Effective Employment of Tactical Aerospace Power in Support of the Joint Task Force Commander." Maxwell Air Force Base, AL: Air University, March 2002. In Defense Technical Information Center, http://www.dtic.mil/dtic/tr/fulltext/u2/a420442.pdf (accessed September 13, 2012).

Goure, Daniel. "The Army Is Ready To Fight, But Can DoD Get It There?" Lexington Institute Early Warning Blog, article posted September 20, 2012. http://www.lexingtoninstitute.org/the-army-is-ready-to-fight-but-can-dod-get-it-there-?a=1&c=1171 (accessed September 22, 2012).

Grange, David L., Huba Wass de Czege, Rich Liebert, Chuck Jarnot, Al Hubner, and Mike Sparks. *Air-Mech-Strike. Asymmetrical Maneuver Warfare for the 21st Century*. Paducah, KY: Turner Publications, 2002.

Griffin, Christopher. "Beyond the Joint Force: Preparing for the Next Korean War." *Armed Forces Journal* 145, no. 11 (June 2008): 30-33, 45-46.

Harrison, Todd, and Mark Gunziger. *Strategic Choices: Navigating Austerity*. Washington, DC: Center for Strategic and Budgetary Assessments, 2012.

Hix, Bill, and Mark C. Smith. "Armor's Asymmetric Advantage: Why a Smaller Army Needs Mobile Protected Firepower." *Armed Forces Journal* (October 2012). http://www.armedforcesjournal.com/2012/10/11460231/ (accessed February 24, 2013).

Hoffman, Frank G. "Forcible Entry Is a Strategic Necessity." *Proceedings* 130, no. 11 (November 2004): 2-2. http://web.ebscohost.com/ehost/detail?sid=2781dc5f-b18 4-44c9-a2e4-04d5d616263d%40sessionmgr13&vid=1&hid=8&bdata=JnNpdGU9 ZWhvc3QtbGl2ZSZzY29wZT1zaXRl#db=a2h&AN=15035504 (accessed September 13, 2012).

Huntington, Samuel P. *The Clash of Civilizations and the Remaking of World Order*. New York, NY: Simon & Schuster, 1996.

Kelly, Sean P. "Airborne Assault Forces: The Most Expedient and Practical Forcible Entry Response Available in Today's Contemporary Operating Environment." Newport, RI: Naval War College, May 4, 2012. In Defense Technical Information Center, http://www.dtic.mil/cgi-bin/GetTRDoc?AD=ADA563877& Location=U2&doc=GetTRDoc.pdf (accessed October 22, 2012).

Krepinevich, Andrew F., Jr. "Strategy in a Time of Austerity: Why the Pentagon Should Focus on Assuring Access." *Foreign Affairs* 91, no. 6 (November-December 2012): 58-69.

———. *Seven Deadly Scenarios: A Military Futurist Explores War in the 21st Century*. New York, NY: Bantam Books, 2009.

Kurowski, Franz. *Jump into Hell: German Paratroopers in World War II*. Mechanichsburg, PA: Stackpole Books, 2010.

Lear, Kyle E. "Airborne Joint Forcible Entry: Ensuring Options for U.S. Global Response." Carlisle Barracks, PA: U.S. Army War College, January 20, 2012. In Defense Technical Information Center, http://www.dtic.mil/cgi-bin/GetTRDoc? AD=ADA561401&Location=U2&doc=GetTRDoc.pdf (accessed September 13, 2012).

Macgregor, Douglas A. "Thoughts on Force Design in an Era of Shrinking Defense Budgets." *Joint Force Quarterly* 63 (October 2011): 21-29.

————. *Breaking the Phalanx: A New Design for Landpower in the 21st Century.* Westport, CT: Praeger, 1997.

Matsumura, John, Randall Steeb, John Gordon IV, Thomas J. Herbert, Russell W. Glenn, and Paul Steinberg. *Lightning over Water: Sharpening America's Light Forces for Rapid-Reaction Missions.* Santa Monica, CA: RAND Arroyo Center, 2001.

McMaster, Herbert R. "Continuity versus Change: Thinking about Future Armed Conflict." Lecture, National War College, Washington, DC, February 8, 2013.

Milevski, Lukas. "*Fortissimus Inter Pares:* The Utility of Landpower in Grand Strategy." *Parameters* XLII, no. 2 (Summer 2012): 6-15.

Moulton, J. L. *The Norwegian Campaign of 1940: A Study of Warfare in Three Dimensions.* London, UK: Eyre & Spottiswoode, 1966.

Nair, V. K. *War in the Gulf: Lessons for the Third World.* New Delhi, India: Lancer International, 1991.

Norman, Albert. *Operation Overlord, Design and Reality: The Allied Invasion of Western Europe.* Westport, CT: Greenwood Press, 1952.

Obama, Barack. *Sustaining U.S. Global Leadership: Priorities for 21st Century Defense.* Washington, DC: Government Printing Office, January 3, 2012.

————. *National Security Strategy.* Washington, DC: Government Printing Office, May 2010. http://www.whitehouse.gov/sites/default/files/rss_viewer/national_security _strategy.pdf (accessed September 14, 2012).

Phillips, R. Cody. *Operation Just Cause: The Incursion into Panama.* Carlisle, PA: U.S. Army Center for Military History, 2004.

Rakocy, Jason G., and Robert Kruger, Jr. *Joint Forcible Entry Warfighter Experiment (JFEWE) 2011 Final Report.* Fort Benning, GA: U.S. Army Maneuver Battle Lab, 2011.

Robertson, Terence. *Dieppe: The Shame and the Glory.* Boston, MA: Little, Brown, 1962.

Roughhead, Gary and Kori Schake. *National Defense in a Time of Change.* Washington, DC: Brookings Institution, February 2013. http://www.brookings.edu/~/media/ research/files/papers/2013/02/us%20national%20defense%20changes/thp_roughe addiscpaper.pdf (accessed March 29, 2013).

Scowcroft, Brent. Foreword to *Power and Responsibility: Building International Order in an Era of Transnational Threats,* by Bruce Jones, Carlos Pascual, and Stephen John Stedman. Washington, DC: Brookings Institution Press, 2009.

Singer, Peter W. "Sequestration and What It Would Do to U.S. Military Power." Time Magazine Battleland Blog, article posted September 24, 2012. http://nation.time.com/2012/09/24/sequestration-and-what-it-would-do-to-u-s-military-power/ (accessed March 3, 2013).

Stiner, Carl. "Operation Just Cause." Lecture, Joint Forces Staff College, Norfolk, VA, March 26, 2013.

Stiner, Carl, and Daniel R. Schroeder. "The Army and Joint Forcible Entry." *Army* 59, no. 11 (November 2009): 19-20.

Sutherland, Christopher L. "Joint Seabasing and Joint Vision 2020." Quantico, VA: U.S. Marine Corps Command and Staff College, Marine Corps University, April 24, 2009. In Defense Technical Information Center, http://oai.dtic.mil/oai/oai?verb=getRecord&metadataPrefix=html& identifier=ADA510839 (accessed October 22, 2012).

Tucker, Jonathan B. *War of Nerves: Chemical Warfare from World War I to al-Qeada.* New York, NY: Pantheon Books, 2006.

United States Office of the Under Secretary of Defense for Acquisition, Technology, and Logistics. "Armed Forces Strength Figures for October 31, 2012." October 2012. http://siadapp.dmdc.osd.mil/personnel/MILITARY/ms0.pdf (accessed February 17, 2013).

U.S. Army Training and Doctrine Command. *The U.S. Army Capstone Concept*, TRADOC Pam 525-3-0. Fort Eustis, VA: U.S. Army Capabilities Integration Center, December 19, 2012.

————. *Gaining and Maintaining Access: An Army-Marine Corps Concept.* Fort Eustis, VA and Quantico, VA: U.S. Army Capabilities Integration Center and U.S. Marine Corps Combat Development Command, March 2012.

————. Deputy Chief of Staff, G2. "Challenges to the Capabilities of the U.S. Army in 2020." White paper, Fort Monroe, VA, January 17, 2011.

U.S. Joint Chiefs of Staff. *Joint Forcible Entry Operations.* Joint Publication 3-18. Washington, DC: U.S. Joint Chiefs of Staff, November 27, 2012.

———. *Joint Logistics Over-The-Shore.* Joint Publication 4-01.6. Washington, DC: U.S. Joint Chiefs of Staff, November 27, 2012.

———. *Capstone Concept for Joint Operations: Joint Force 2020.* Washington, DC: U.S. Joint Chiefs of Staff, September 10, 2012.

———. *Decade of War, Volume 1: Enduring Lessons from the Past Decade of Operations.* Suffolk, VA: Joint Center for Operational Analysis, June 15, 2012.

———. *Joint Operational Access Concept.* Version 1.0. Washington, DC: U.S. Joint Chiefs of Staff, January 17, 2012.

———. *Joint Operations.* Joint Publication 3-0. Washington, DC: U.S. Joint Chiefs of Staff, August 11, 2011.

———. *Department of Defense Dictionary of Military and Associated Terms.* Joint Publication 1-02. Washington, DC: U.S. Joint Chiefs of Staff, November 8, 2010, (as amended through May 15, 2011).

———. *The National Military Strategy of the United States of America 2011: Redefining America's Military Leadership.* Washington, DC: U.S. Joint Chiefs of Staff, February 8, 2011.

———. *Amphibious Operations.* Joint Publication 3-02. Washington, DC: U.S. Joint Chiefs of Staff, August 10, 2009.

U.S. Joint Forces Command. *The Joint Operating Environment 2010.* Suffolk, VA: U.S. Joint Forces Command, February 18, 2010.

U.S. Navy Fleet Forces Command. *Concept for Employment of Current Seabasing Capabilities: Integrating Seabasing Capabilities Into Exercises and Experiments.* Norfolk, VA: U.S. Fleet Forces Command, June 29, 2010.

Van Tol, Jan, Mark Gunzinger, Andrew Krepinevich, and Jim Thomas. *AirSea Battle: A Point of Departure Operational Concept.* Washington, DC: Center for Strategic and Budgetary Assessments, 2010.

Work, Robert O. and Frank. G. Hoffman. "Hitting the Beach in the 21st Century." *Proceedings* 136, no. 11 (November 2010): 1,293. http://www.usni.org/magazines/proceedings/2010-11/hitting-beach-21st-century (accessed October 22, 2012).

Wylie, J. C. *Military Strategy: A General Theory of Power Control.* Annapolis, MD: Naval Institute Press, 1989.